"Written by a sufferer who is also a skilled theol[...]
is honest, tender, full of grace, and burst[...]
of God's Word. With story after story[...]
how the Bible accurately portrays our su[...]
the midst of them. Since suffering really [...] ...erience
between the 'already' and the 'not yet,' th[...] ...in getting and
living with. I found it to be enormously hel[...] ...u you will too."

Paul David Tripp, President, Paul Tripp Ministries; author, *What
Did You Expect?*

"Dr. Ryken is serving as the president of one of the most important Christian institutions of our time. Even in my work in the Middle East, I have been blessed by Wheaton College through my ongoing relationships with professors there and also through the many Wheaton graduates who have worked with me over the years. Dr. Ryken is there through both good times and difficult times, always leading with integrity and wisdom, so that Wheaton College can truly be 'For Christ and His Kingdom.' In this book, Dr. Ryken shows his characteristic integrity in his ability to be vulnerable before others in order that they might find solace in Jesus Christ. I am so pleased to fully endorse this book, written by a man I hold in highest esteem."

Canon Andrew White, Vicar Emeritus, St. George's Church,
Baghdad, Iraq; President, Foundation for Relief and Reconciliation
in the Middle East

"When trouble comes, most Christians want to escape it, deny or divorce it, or medicate or avoid it—we do everything but actually try to *live* with it! Thankfully, Dr. Ryken takes great pains in this remarkable book to show us how to live gladly and gloriously through our troubles. Rather than take us on a detour around our hardships, he serves as our guide *through* them. If you are finding it hard to 'welcome trials as friends,' *this* is the book for you."

Joni Eareckson Tada, Founder and CEO, Joni and Friends
International Disability Center

"Few books present both comfort and challenge like *When Trouble Comes*. Dr. Ryken weaves his own story with the likes of Ruth, David, and Paul to illuminate God's path to resilience. You will gain practical steps to hope when your own soul is troubled and a clear call to action when you witness pain in the world."

Lisa Beamer, author, *Let's Roll*

"*When Trouble Comes* is a profound book for people in profound trouble. We don't need to go looking for it, of course. Sooner or later, some life-altering catastrophe that only God can get us through crashes into our lives. And God does help us, very wonderfully, as we fall into his loving arms. Dr. Ryken, a man I highly respect, gently shows us from the Bible how God cares for us when our very lives are on the line. May the Lord bless you as you read this encouraging book, even as he has blessed me."

Raymond C. Ortlund Jr., Lead Pastor, Immanuel Church, Nashville, Tennessee

"As much as we hate to admit it, trouble inevitably marks every one of our lives. The Preacher was right when he wrote in Ecclesiastes that all our 'days are full of sorrow.' *When Trouble Comes* assumes that trouble will come—and not just to people who are living in rebellion against God, but to those, even especially to those, who are seeking to live for God's glory. With deep wisdom and broad scriptural insight, Dr. Ryken identifies the sources of our troubles and calls us to faith in the Son who endured suffering and enters into all our sorrows."

Elyse M. Fitzpatrick, counselor; speaker; author, *Found in Him*

"All believers suffer, and sometimes we suffer in agonizing ways. Dr. Ryken helps us understand suffering from God's perspective by telling the stories of biblical figures who endured suffering. His own story, related at the beginning of the book, is compelling and encouraging. We need energy and fuel to make it through the hard times, and Dr. Ryken gives us that fuel in this biblically saturated book."

Thomas R. Schreiner, James Buchanan Harrison Professor of New Testament Interpretation and Associate Dean of the School of Theology, The Southern Baptist Theological Seminary

WHEN TROUBLE COMES

PHIL RYKEN

WHEATON, ILLINOIS

Library of Congress Cataloging-in-Publication Data

Names: Ryken, Philip Graham, 1966–
Title: When trouble comes / Phil Ryken.
Description: Wheaton: Crossway, 2016. | Includes bibliographical references and index. | Description based on print version record and CIP data provided by publisher; resource not viewed.
Identifiers: LCCN 2015045055 (print) | LCCN 2015035082 (ebook) | ISBN 9781433549748 (pdf) | ISBN 9781433549755 (mobi) | ISBN 9781433549762 (epub) | ISBN 9781433549731 (tp)
Subjects: LCSH: Suffering—Biblical teaching. | Suffering—Religious Aspects—Christianity.
Classification: LCC BS680.S854 (print) | LCC BS680.S854 R95 2016 (ebook) | DDC 231/.8—dc23
LC record available at http://lccn.loc.gov/2015045055

Crossway is a publishing ministry of Good News Publishers.

VP		26	25	24	23	22	21	20	19	18	17
15	14	13	12	11	10	9	8	7	6	5	4	3

To everyone who has ever prayed for
me when I was in trouble,
and to my gracious Lord, Jesus Christ,
who has considered my trouble and
forgiven all my sins (Ps. 25:18).

Contents

Nobody Knows the Trouble I've Seen

(Psalm 37:39–40)

It was the spring semester of the academic year, and I was in trouble. Real trouble. Over the course of several long and difficult weeks, I fell deeper and deeper into discouragement until eventually there were days when I wondered if I had the will to live.

At the time, most people didn't know anything about it, which is why I am borrowing my prologue title from an old African-American spiritual: "Nobody Knows the Trouble I've Seen."

I don't talk about myself much in my books and public messages. My main purpose is to talk about Jesus. But sometimes talking about me can help me tell other people about Jesus, and this is one of those times.

In this small book, I tell the stories of men and women from the Bible who were in all kinds of trouble—people such as Isaiah, Elijah, Ruth, and Paul. They were weighed down by guilt and shame, suffered the death of loved ones, had family crises, or went through other painful trials that tested their faith. For some, the trial was absolutely a matter of life and death.

I've called the book *When Trouble Comes*, and what I want to show is how God helped these people. What made the difference for these men and women of true faith? What did they do when trouble came?

I'm interested in this for my own benefit, and also for yours—because I know that you will be in trouble, too. In fact, you may be in trouble right now. Even if nobody knows the trouble you've seen, you are weighed down by guilt and shame, grieving the loss of a relationship, or facing an uncertain future. And if you're not in trouble now, cheer up! You will be, sooner or later. And when this happens, it will help you immensely to know what godly people do when trouble comes.

But before I tell you any stories from the Bible, I want to tell you some of my story, and especially what helped me make it through. I won't tell you all of the reasons why I was in trouble, because some of those reasons are connected to other people's stories, and I need to respect their privacy. But I will tell you what it felt like to be in trouble, and how God rescued me. To borrow a few lines from the English poet and preacher George Herbert, "I live to show his power, who once did bring my joys to weep, and now my griefs to sing."[1]

The Troubles I've Seen

In a strange way, what happened to me could have been an answer to prayer. Someone very close to me—someone I love more than life itself—was going through a time of real trouble. These troubles came with feelings of such terrifying fear and painful sadness that life no longer seemed worth living. These intense sufferings were far beyond anything I had ever experienced in my own life. So I asked God to lift her burden and, insofar as possible, to let me carry it instead. "Lord, she's too little," I said. "She doesn't understand what's happening to her. Let me take whatever pain you choose to give. In Jesus's name."

Sometimes I wish the Lord *wouldn't* answer my prayers, but this time maybe he did. All I know is that in the weeks and months that followed, while my beloved's burden gradually lifted, my joy was turned to sorrow.

My day job as the president of Wheaton College has plenty of challenges to begin with. I'm tempted to agree with the scholar from the University of Virginia who studied leadership for higher education and concluded that the American college presidency is "beyond the ability of anyone to do the job."[2] Balancing the budget, handling delicate personnel matters, caring for students in danger, facing legal accusations, responding to angry letters, trying to raise tens of millions of dollars, making crucial hiring decisions, handling attacks from the media—it's all in a day's work. Ordinarily, these are all burdens I can bear without losing too much sleep; otherwise, I couldn't do the job. And, thankfully, there are lots of other people who help me carry all the burdens every day.

But my beloved's suffering affected me very deeply. And,

in the wise providence of God, I faced other troubles, too—heavy burdens that are too private to share in detail: broken relationships, attacks on my character, painful experiences from the past. It wasn't the best semester for me to go through my 360-degree performance review and get honest feedback (the good, the bad, and the ugly) about my leadership from hundreds of faculty, staff members, alumni, and students.

All of this left me feeling sad and sometimes anxious. There were nights when I had trouble sleeping and mornings when I woke up hours before dawn. It was hard to get up and face the day. There were some mornings when I cried most of the time I was getting ready.

I doubt I was very good company. My problems were taking so much emotional energy that it was hard for me to be with people for very many hours at a time. I remember that on Easter Sunday, of all days, when we had a house full of guests, I needed to go and be alone several times just to make it through the day.

My wife, Lisa, and I went to the doctor, and when the staff ran through their checklist for emotional health, I scored really badly, which was humbling. I began to struggle with whether God loved me or not—another new experience. When I read his promises, I doubted whether I qualified. I would try to take comfort in a verse such as Psalm 86:2, which says, "Preserve my life, for I am godly; save your servant, who trusts in you." The problem, of course, was that I'm not all that godly to begin with, and I was having trouble trusting the Lord, so I had no guarantee that God would save me.

I could tell that I was in a downward spiral. One day I said to myself: "You know, I understand why people kill themselves.

This is how they feel. It seems like the only way out." A few days later, I started to wonder how I would end it all, if, you know . . . It wasn't a thought I wanted to have, but Satan was after me. Give him any little chance and he will take it. Things were moving in a bad direction, and at the rate they were going, how long would it be before I was in real danger?

A Normal Part of Life

Those are some of the troubles I've seen—not all of them, by any means, but some of what I experienced one spring. I suppose that now I need to change my title to, "Everybody Knows the Trouble I've Seen."

What I want to tell you, though, is that God did not abandon me, but rescued me. My loving heavenly Father and my Lord and Savior, Jesus Christ, together with the helping, comforting Holy Spirit, brought me safely through. I can't say that my trials are over or that feelings of despair will never return. But I can give the testimony that David gave and say, "The salvation of the righteous is from the LORD; he is their stronghold in the time of trouble" (Ps. 37:39).

Would you like to know some of the things that helped me? The first was this: I knew that what I was going through was totally and completely normal. I can't ever remember struggling before with serious doubts about God's love or with feelings of despair. But that is unusual. The bitterness I briefly tasted is something that most Christians go through sooner or later, and that some Christians struggle with for a lifetime.

I know this from the experience of close friends and family members. I also know it from the history of the church. To give just one example, the great nineteenth-century London preacher Charles Spurgeon struggled with depression over decades of ministry. Preachers he respected told their congregations not to "give way to feelings of depression." But Spurgeon said: "If those who blame quite so furiously could once know what depression is, they would think it cruel to scatter blame where comfort is needed. There are experiences of the children of God which are full of spiritual darkness; and I am almost persuaded that those of God's servants who have been most highly favored have, nevertheless, suffered more times of darkness than others."[3]

We see the same thing in Scripture. Job was tempted to curse God and die. Isaiah was undone. David was downcast. Elijah asked God to take his life. These men were not weak or rebellious; they were simply weighed down by the burdens of life and ministry. Even Jesus went through a dark night of the soul, when he wondered if there was an alternative to the cross, and an afternoon of agony, when he felt forsaken by the Father.

All of this leads me to accept seasons of doubt, discouragement, and depression as a normal part of life in a fallen world. When trouble comes, this does not mean that I am a bad Christian. Nor does it mean that God is against me, although sometimes I may feel that way. In my time of trouble, it helped immensely to know that I was going through something that happens to most of God's beloved children.

Another thing that helped me was trying to live a normal, everyday life. There were days when this was extremely difficult, but I did it as well as I could. I didn't have much appetite, but I made sure that I ate something healthy every day.

I pushed myself to get physical exercise, even when I didn't have a lot of energy. Praise God for intramural soccer, which helped save my life. Getting regular exercise took my focus off my problems. It strengthened me both physically and emotionally.

I tried to be present with my children: recitals, concerts, baseball games, rides to school, family dinners, bedtime. Some of the memories will stay with me for a lifetime. One of my daughters and I sang hymns and praise songs together in her bedroom when our hearts were both breaking—some of my best worship experiences ever. Another daughter joined me for early morning bird walks in the springtime. I saw God's beauty in the swallows on the wing, his joy in the warblers singing in the sunshine, his wisdom in the great horned owls brooding in the oak trees. What is more, I was blessed by my daughter's companionship— her ministry of presence to me.

I went to worship—church on Sundays and college chapel services during the week. I didn't always feel very much like worshiping—Christians don't always—but that was another place where God met me. Hymns and songs that expressed God's grace for my need became especially meaningful, such as these words from the German hymn writer Johann Franck:

> Though the earth be shaking,
> ev'ry heart be quaking,
> Jesus calms my fear.
> Lightnings flash and thunders crash;
> yet, though sin and hell assail me,
> Jesus will not fail me.[4]

And, of course, I did my work at Wheaton College five or six days a week. I didn't quit, but kept up the ordinary routines of daily life: food and drink, work and play, family and worship.

All of those things helped, because they are all part of God's design for our flourishing.

A Friend's a Friend Forever

Friends helped me, too, and one of the reasons they were able to help is that I shared what was happening in my life. I didn't share everything with everybody, of course. After all, who would even *want* to know all my troubles? But I told people what I was going through. I talked to my parents. I spoke with some of my closest friends. I shared my struggles with other Christian college presidents. And, of course, every day I talked my trials over with my best friend, the girl from Colorado with whom I fell in love when we were both in college.

Very importantly, I made sure that Wheaton's trustees knew how much pressure I was under. This was important for me, and also for the college. I need to respect the leadership that God has placed over me, which includes not pretending that everything is going well when it isn't. Some of the burdens I was bearing also needed pastoral oversight. So Lisa and I turned to couples in ministry who have known us for a long time and will still love us a long time after we leave Wheaton.

The point is that burdens are never meant to be carried alone. If you are having a problem, please tell a brother or sister you trust and someone who has the responsibility to care for you. This is an important part of healthy life in the body of Christ.

I was helped by small kindnesses, such as the text my son Josh sent me, offering to help me in any way that he could, or the sunshine card the ladies in my office left on my desk.

One afternoon, when I was having despairing thoughts, I

stepped out of a meeting to be alone for a few minutes. In the providence of God, one of my best and oldest friends—Jon Dennis, who is the pastor of Chicago's Holy Trinity Church—called right then to find out how I was doing. I told him that I was losing the will to live. That in itself helped put things in perspective and loosened the power of self-destructive thoughts.

But what made an even bigger difference is that my friend told me that he loved me. I knew this was true. We had grown up together, and he had always been a faithful friend. But it made a big difference in my life for him to tell me right at that moment that he loved me, which he wouldn't have done unless he had known how much trouble I was in, which he wouldn't have known unless I had told him.

My friends also prayed for me, which is another thing that helped, a lot. When trouble comes, nothing helps like the power of prayer.

Many people pray for me all the time, which is humbling. People I don't even know have a commitment to Wheaton College that calls them to prayer. I get cards and letters from people who tell me they pray for me daily or weekly. Every Thursday, a group of godly women gathers a few blocks from campus to spend a morning in prayer for Wheaton College, which makes a huge difference.

But in my time of trouble, I needed even more prayer, and I also needed to know that people were praying for me. I missed a meeting with my cabinet, and later I learned that they spent an extended time in prayer for my protection. The trustees were praying for me, too, and many of them sent personal notes of encouragement. One night, my mother and father laid their hands on me. As he prayed, my father mentioned what King Hezekiah did when the Assyrians surrounded Jerusalem and sent a letter that threatened the city's total destruction. Hezekiah took the letter, spread it before the Lord, and prayed that God would save him (2 Kings 19:14–19). In the same way, my father took my troubles and spread them before the Lord in prayer.

All of these prayers helped, but some of the deepest encouragement came from my old college classmates. Most of them knew only some of the troubles I was facing, but that was enough to mobilize them for intercession. My freshman roommate, Steve Snezek, wrote from Montana and told me that he would pray for me. Jimmy Favino, who teaches high school English in Philadelphia, sent me an email to say that he was going to spend the next day in fasting and prayer, just for me. Lisa and I learned that our precious friends the Nussbaums and the Garretts were meeting on Sunday nights to pray for us.

I can hardly express how much it means to me that so many people cared enough about me to pray. I've mentioned some of their names here to honor their friendship, but also to show that when real trouble comes, we need real people to help us. When I was in deep distress, my friends covered me with petitions and benedictions. Their righteous prayers were a powerful instrument of God's grace in my life. And so I wonder: What friend in trouble needs my prayers? And who needs yours?

Meanwhile, I was praying, too. In my prayers, I told God exactly what I was thinking, just like Job did when he was afflicted. Sometimes I didn't know what to ask or couldn't find the words to form an intelligible petition. I could only say, "Help me, Jesus" or "Son of David, have mercy on me!" Or I could only groan, literally. But the Holy Spirit understands our inner struggles so well that he is able to translate our groanings into prayer. "We do not know what to pray for as we ought," Scripture says, "but the Spirit himself intercedes for us with groanings too deep for words" (Rom. 8:26). Sometimes I wondered what sense the Holy Spirit could make of my anguished soul. I only know that when trouble came, he turned my groans into prayers at the throne of my Father's grace.

The Last Word

Here is one more thing that helped me: God's Word, the Bible, the Scriptures of the Old and New Testaments. I treasured the verses that my mother shared with me from the psalms of David: "On the day I called, you answered me; my strength of soul you increased"; "Though I walk in the midst of trouble, you preserve my life"; "The LORD will fulfill his purpose for me; your steadfast love, O LORD, endures forever" (Ps. 138:3, 7, 8). Some of my best memories are the times that Lisa and I had in bed late at night, when she would read psalms over me until I fell asleep, quieting my anxious spirit with the true words of God.

One of the main ways that God becomes an ever-present help to us in times of trouble is by speaking his truth to our minds and hearts, which is why I wrote this book. I agree with Spurgeon's claim that "the worst forms of depression are cured when Holy Scripture is believed."[5] So I want people to see from Scripture the help that God has for all of us in times of trouble.

I know that you will be in trouble, too. It might even happen today. You will suffer the sudden loss of someone you love. You will struggle with a sin that you can't seem to get rid of. You will experience the pain of a broken relationship. There will be problems in your family that no one can fix. You will have to give up one of your dreams. You will wonder how God can provide for your needs. You will have serious doubts about things that always seemed so simple to believe. You will be overwhelmed by the pressures of work or school. You might be tempted to hate yourself, or even to despair of life itself.

What will you do when trouble comes?

The things that helped me will also help you, maybe even more than you know. They are the basic things of life: a good night's sleep, a healthy meal, going to church, talking with a faithful friend, meeting with God through prayer, and meditating on his Word.

The reason these things all help is because they are gifts from our loving Savior, Jesus Christ. When I tell you what helped me in my time of trouble, I am really telling you all the ways that Jesus helped me. Our bodies are the gift of his wisdom and creative power. Whenever we sit down to eat a good meal, we are hosted by his providence. Work is a gift from Jesus, too. Play is another gift, and then afterward a good night of rest. Jesus has given us one another to encourage our souls, especially in corporate worship. He has sent his Spirit to help us pray. Most of all, he has given us life through his death and resurrection. It is all by God's grace to us in Jesus Christ.

I don't know what trouble you've seen. But I believe that what David said is true: "The salvation of the righteous is from the LORD; he is their stronghold in the time of trouble. The LORD helps them and delivers them; he . . . saves them, because they take refuge in him" (Ps. 37:39–40). By the grace of God, this is my testimony, in Jesus's name. And I so very much want it to be your testimony, too.

1

"Woe Is Me!"

Isaiah's Sin and Guilt

(Isaiah 6:1–8)

It was the year that King Uzziah died, and Isaiah was in trouble. Real trouble. He wasn't the only one, either. The entire nation of Israel was guilty of grievous sin against a holy God. As a result, the people were about to fall under divine condemnation, Isaiah included. So he cried out and said: "Woe is me! For I am lost; for I am a man of unclean lips, and I dwell in the midst of a people of unclean lips; for my eyes have seen the King, the LORD of hosts!" (Isa. 6:5).

Woe to Them!

To understand how much trouble Isaiah was in, it helps to know that he was a prophet. Therefore, he was the mouthpiece of

God—a man who spoke words of blessing and judgment on behalf of the living God. Some of his words—not a lot, but some—were favorable. Isaiah promised that light would shine out of the darkness, that a virgin would conceive and bear a son, that those who waited on the Lord would rise up like eagles, and that a righteous servant would be crushed for our iniquities and wounded for our transgressions.

Yet many of Isaiah's words were weighted with the judgment of God. One of the best places to see this is in the chapter that comes right before the passage where Isaiah finds himself in trouble.

Frankly, Isaiah 6 is one of those familiar Bible passages that most Christians don't know as well as they think they do. Many people know verse 4: "Holy, holy, holy is the LORD of hosts; the whole earth is full of his glory!" Many also know verse 8, which is one of the great missionary texts in the Bible. It's the kind of text that often shows up on plaques and T-shirts: "Here am I! Send me!" (NIV). The words are very inspiring. But how many people know the verses that come right before this or the ones that come after?

To understand a text, we have to know the context. And when we turn back to Isaiah 5, we find the prophet pronouncing judgment against the people of God. He talks about a carefully tended vine that would not bear fruit, using it as a metaphor for Israel: God's people were not producing good spiritual fruit.

So Isaiah said "Woe" to them. Six times! He lamented their unjust affluence: "Woe to those who join house to house, who add field to field" (Isa. 5:8). He condemned their drunkenness: "Woe to those who . . . run after strong drink, who tarry late into the evening as wine inflames them!" (v. 11). He criticized their dishonesty: "Woe to those who draw iniquity with cords of falsehood" (v. 18). He rebuked their moral relativism: "Woe to those who call evil good and good evil" (v. 20). He chastised their intellectual pride: "Woe to those who are wise in their own eyes" (v. 21). And he indicted their injustice: "Woe to those who . . . deprive the innocent of his right!" (vv. 22–23).

As we review Isaiah's lamentable list of woes, we may well wonder what the prophet would say to us. Maybe we would prefer not to know, because most of us do not particularly enjoy having our sins exposed. But in all likelihood, Isaiah would say some of the same things to us that he said to ancient Israel. Woe to us for using our wealth to multiply selfish privilege, for abusing alcohol and other pleasures, for bending the truth to improve our image, or for shrinking the ethical teaching of Scripture to make it fit better with our sinful desires. And woe to us for thinking that Isaiah 5 is mainly for someone else—someone we hope will finally listen—rather than realizing that God is speaking to us. We should not be "wise in our own eyes," as Isaiah describes it, but admit that we, too, do not have it all together spiritually yet.

Woe Is Me!

This brings us to one of the most remarkable aspects of this passage. As noted above, Isaiah pronounces six woes in chapter 5: "Woe to this person," "Woe to that person," and "Woe to those people over there." To make his prophecy complete, we might expect him to pronounce a seventh woe. After all, seven is the biblical number that makes things complete.

And, in fact, Isaiah *does* pronounce a seventh woe! It is the famous woe in chapter 6, verse 5: "Woe is me! For I am lost; for I am a man of unclean lips, and I dwell in the midst of a people of unclean lips." Isaiah could not simply go around saying "Woe to you" all the time. He could not simply set everyone else straight and comment on everyone else's sin without ever confessing his own. No, in the year that King Uzziah died, Isaiah came to a point of total honesty about the fact that he was as big a sinner as everyone else—maybe bigger.

Amazingly, Isaiah did this in the one area of life that he had most completely surrendered to God. If people in Israel had asked, "Is there anyone we can count on to tell the truth?" the answer would have been, "Isaiah the prophet." In fact, the man probably would have said it himself. "There are other areas of life where I struggle," Isaiah might have said, "but if there is one part of my body that is totally dedicated to God, it is my mouth." The man was a prophet, after all, which meant that he was a spokesperson for God.

But then Isaiah realized that he was a foul-mouthed sinner, too. Suddenly it occurred to him that *he* was a man who used bad language, who employed his rhetorical skill to get people to do what he wanted, who said something critical when he could have said something beneficial. And at the very moment the prophet recognized this, he said: "Woe is me! I am utterly undone, because I have discovered that my mouth is just as filthy as anyone else's."

Isaiah's confession is a good word for anyone who makes critical comments, which includes most of us. This is always a temptation at work, in church, on a college campus, in a family, and pretty much everywhere else. When critical thinking is not consecrated by humility, it becomes a critical spirit. So we become critical of others' performance, background, style, or sense of humor. We condemn the way they think, what they say, and the choices they make. There is always someone to criticize—someone who doesn't have it together the way we do. Most of us will keep on criticizing until God saves us the way he saved Isaiah: by showing us that our attitude is a much bigger problem than whatever we think is wrong with everyone else.

Aleksandr Solzhenitsyn came to a similar place of recognition in *The Gulag Archipelago*, his famous exposé of the evils of the Soviet Union. The Nobel laureate anticipated that some readers would expect him to draw a clear and simple distinction between the good people and the evil people. Solzhenitsyn replied: "If only it were all so simple! If only there were evil people somewhere insidiously committing evil deeds, and it were necessary only to separate them from the rest of us and destroy them. But the line dividing good and evil cuts through the heart of every human being . . ."[1]

It was not wrong for Isaiah to pronounce God's judgment. He was a prophet, so that was his job. But his biggest issue was his own sin. There was not one single area of his life that he could say was perfect—not even the areas that he tried the hardest to offer to God. So before he could go out and do what God was calling him to do, Isaiah had to come clean and say, "Woe is me!"

The astronomer Johannes Kepler also expressed conviction and confession. Kepler had long dedicated the best of his intellectual powers to the exploration of the universe. He had done so with the explicit purpose of bringing glory to God. But even his calling as a scientist came with unavoidable temptations. So Kepler offered this marvelous prayer:

> If I have been enticed into brashness
> by the wonderful beauty of thy works,
> or if I have loved my own glory among men,
> while advancing in work destined for thy glory,
> gently and mercifully pardon me:
> and finally,
> deign graciously to cause that these demonstrations
> may lead to thy glory and to the salvation of souls,
> and nowhere be an obstacle to that.
> Amen.[2]

It is worth asking: "What sin do I need to confess?" Answering truthfully may be the first step toward your salvation. Perhaps you need to say, "Woe is me, for I am the person who likes people to think more highly of me than they should." "Woe is me, for I am the person who tears people down instead of building them up." "Woe is me, for I have firm moral convictions in some areas, but I like to make exceptions when I would rather do my own thing." Or "Woe is me, for I am as sinful as Isaiah was, if not worse."

Totally Awesome!

To fully appreciate how much trouble Isaiah was in, we also need to know what he was seeing at that moment. Here we come to some of the most awe-inspiring verses in the entire Bible:

> In the year that King Uzziah died I saw the Lord sitting upon a throne, high and lifted up; and the train of his robe

filled the temple. Above him stood the seraphim. Each had six wings; with two he covered his face, and with two he covered his feet, and with two he flew. And one called to another and said: "Holy, holy, holy is the LORD of hosts; the whole earth is full of his glory!" And the foundations of the thresholds shook at the voice of him who called, and the house was filled with smoke. (Isa. 6:1–4)

Everything about this scene is totally awesome. God is awesome. Here we see Isaiah's vision of Almighty God—specifically, God the Son. We know this because when John referred to Isaiah's ministry, he said that the prophet saw the glory of Jesus Christ (John 12:41). Isaiah saw the awesomeness of God in the person of his only Son.

The prophet also saw God's throne, which is just as awesome. I know thrones are awesome because when students participate in chapel worship at Wheaton College, they hesitate to sit in the big chair. People leading worship at Wheaton sit in large, fairly ornate chairs on the stage of Edman Chapel. I call them "the Narnia chairs" because they look like the thrones from Cair Paravel, the magnificent castle in the Chronicles of Narnia by C. S. Lewis. For some reason, people always seem to be in awe of the big chair; they know it's not for them. So imagine what Isaiah felt when he went into the throne room of heaven and saw God's throne "high and lifted up." Jesus Christ sits on the highest of all thrones. He is elevated and exalted.

His robe is equally awesome. Isaiah saw its train fill the temple. Think of a bride on her wedding day, with her beautiful dress trailing down the aisle. Now imagine her bridal train filling the aisle, spilling out into the church, pressing up against the walls, and piling up towards the ceiling. When Isaiah saw the train of the robe of the Lord who sits on the throne of God, it filled the temple. That's awesome!

God's angels are awesome, and Isaiah saw them as well—the mighty seraphim. These majestic six-winged beings—which we would be tempted to worship the moment we saw them—are so overwhelmed by the greater holiness of God that they cover themselves: two wings over their faces and two wings over their feet. And with their other two wings, they hover in the holy presence of God.

What these angels say is awesome as well: "Holy, holy, holy is the LORD of hosts; the whole earth is full of his glory!" Repetition is the Bible's way of adding exclamation marks. So when the angels repeat the word *holy*, and then repeat it again, they are testifying to the absolutely perfect, totally pristine holiness of God, bearing witness to the holiness of the Father, the Son, and the Holy Spirit.

Isaiah heard an awesome sound—voices so mighty that they shook the foundations of heaven. There were awesome smells, too, because the house of God was filled with smoke. This was a total sensory experience of the awesomeness of God.

Here is something else that is absolutely awesome: everything that Isaiah experienced is happening right now in the throne room of the universe. We know this because when the doors of heaven were opened for the apostle John, as recorded in his famous Revelation, he saw living creatures worshiping God the Son. "Each of them [has] six wings," John tells us, "and day and night they never cease to say, 'Holy, holy, holy, is the Lord God Almighty, who was and is and is to come!'" (Rev. 4:8).

Sound familiar? This is the same thing that Isaiah heard, because it is what the seraphim are always saying, which is totally awesome! Apparently, there are angels whose eternal employment is to worship God in all of his holiness. They have been doing this since the day they were created. They are doing it now, and they will do it forever—thereby offering God an infinity of holy praise.

The Morality Gap

Can we even imagine what it was like for Isaiah to experience this? Even if we can't, we can see how much trouble he was in. Isaiah 6 is the juxtaposition of two absolute extremes. Two things were coming together: the awesome holiness of God and the woeful guiltiness of his prophet. Nothing is holier than the triune God, and nothing is unholier than the lips of a man who has been going around telling everyone else how unholy they are without confessing his own sin.

When he stood in that throne room and realized that he was caught in the middle, Isaiah was completely undone, totally shattered, absolutely broken, and utterly ruined. All he could say was: "Woe is me! For I am lost."

It is wise for each of us to consider whether we have come to a similar place in our own lives, making a complete confession and admitting without reservation that we are sinners in the sight of God. Isaiah's trouble was not just this sin or that sin; it was his very identity as a sinner. He would never be holy enough for God. Anyone who catches even one glimpse of God's true holiness knows immediately that he or she is in deadly peril.

So let me ask: Have you ever been where Isaiah was when he found himself woefully lost? Have you seen enough of the holiness of God to know that you are a guilty sinner? It's not just the bad things we did that we still feel guilty about; the bad things we do that we can't stop doing; or all the good things we should do but don't. No, it's the trouble we're in as the sinners we are.

Our Part: Confessing Our Sins

So what should we do when we're in this kind of trouble? What can be done about our most basic problem, which is sin and guilt?

The first thing to do, of course, is to admit it, which is what Isaiah did. He didn't try to defend himself. He didn't come up with a lot of excuses. He didn't say, "Lord, I know I'm a sinner, but I just want to point out that there are some other people around here who break your covenant a lot more than I do." He didn't try to claim that his good deeds outnumbered his bad deeds or that he always had good intentions, even if he failed to live up to them. No, once he could see the massive canyon that separated him from the pristine holiness of God, he confessed his sin.

Furthermore, he confessed his sin in the one area of life where he had always prided himself on being particularly righteous. As a prophet, he had dedicated his life to speaking the pure words of God. But even there he fell short. So he said, "I am a man of unclean lips" (Isa. 6:5).

Isaiah's example should prompt us to identify the areas of life where we pride ourselves on giving everything to God. Whatever it is—whether it is sports, music, academics, or ministry—there is not one single part of us that is perfectly protected from the stain of sin.

I could give lots of examples from my own life, but here is just one. Some years ago, I was meeting with the interns in our church—young people preparing for ministry—and I shared a list of sins that are particularly tempting for pastors. As I read down the list, I said to myself, "Yeah, these sins are all really tempting for me, too, except maybe that one." The sin that I thought wasn't so tempting for me was cynicism.

I'm an optimist; I try to see the best in everything. So I don't think of myself as a cynic. But guess which sin I've been most convicted of since that night with my interns? Spiritual cynicism. It's tempting for me to criticize a Christian experience that seems shallow to me or that I think people get more excited about than they should.

So here is a challenge for every Christian: take one area of life that you have pretty well dedicated to God and ask the Holy Spirit to convict you of sin right there. It won't take long. Soon you will see that you're in trouble there, too. We're in trouble with sin everywhere. But knowing this is part of God's grace to us, because it gives us a chance to repent. Hopefully, we will do this the way that Isaiah did, when he freely confessed that he was a sinner to the very core. We will say: "O LORD, be gracious to us; we wait for you. Be our arm every morning, our salvation in the time of trouble" (Isa. 33:2).

God's Part: Atoning for Sin

Really, this was the only thing that Isaiah *could* do: confess his sin. Likewise, there is nothing more we can do to solve the great trouble of our guilt than simply to admit our sin. But there is more that God can do, and he does it!

As soon as Isaiah confessed his sin, "one of the seraphim" flew to him. "In his hand" he had "a burning coal that he had taken with tongs from the altar." The angel pressed that blazing ember against Isaiah's lips and said, "Behold, this has touched your lips; your guilt is taken away, and your sin atoned for" (Isa. 6:6–7).

These verses teach us many things about the forgiveness of sin. They teach us that we do not need to wait for God to forgive us; we are forgiven the very moment we repent. When we feel guilty about our sins, we should not delay. Instead, we should run straight to God and make a full confession. God is gracious to forgive. Although he knew how much trouble Isaiah was in—what a woeful sinner he was—he did not destroy him; he saved him! Whatever the sin, when we confess it, God's mercy flies to us the way the angel flew to Isaiah.

This mercy, this forgiveness, is for each and every sin, which is something else we learn from these verses. God offers specific forgiveness for particular sins. In touching the coal to Isaiah's mouth, the seraph dealt precisely with the sin that the prophet had confessed: unclean lips. It must have been excruciating. Notice that the seraph had to use tongs to pick up the coal. What the angel did with the coal was painful but effective, because Isaiah's sin was totally purged. His full confession was followed by complete cleansing.

These verses also tell us that forgiveness is offered on the basis of blood. Notice that the seraph's burning coal came from the altar where sacrifices were made for sin. This is why Isaiah's guilt was taken away and his sin atoned for: a lamb was slain, blood was spilt, a judgment fire was lit, and then, as a result, Isaiah's troubles were over.

Praise God: all of this grace is available to us in Jesus Christ. When we are in trouble because we are guilty (not if, but when), there is a way for us to be saved. The moment we confess our sins, God flies to us with his forgiveness. The Holy Spirit takes the atonement that Jesus accomplished and applies it directly to our sin. Pride, jealousy, lust, greed, theft, dishonesty, prejudice—Jesus dealt with all of our troubling sins on the cross.

Because of the cross, we no longer need to say, "Woe is me!" Instead, we can say, "Thank you, Jesus." Then and only then will we be ready to say what Isaiah said next: "Here I am! Send me."

2

"I've Had Enough"

Elijah's Desperate Depression

(1 Kings 19:1–18)

It was a little while after the spiritual showdown on Mount Carmel, where he had faced off against 450 prophets of Baal, and Elijah was in trouble. Real trouble. Just a few days earlier, the prophet of God had won a complete triumph. His ministry had been vindicated. His enemies had been defeated. His prayers had been answered. Elijah had seen an entire nation turn its heart back to God. But that was then. Now, Elijah was burned out, depressed, suicidal. It was *not* well with the prophet's soul. He sat alone under a solitary tree and said: "I've had enough, Lord. If you want my life, you can have it, because I don't want to go on living even one more day."

A Great Man of God

As Elijah fades to black, we should remember the spiritual accomplishments of this great man of God. In dark and troubled times, Elijah was a burning and shining light for the people of God. Boldly he went to wicked King Ahab and told him that as punishment for his idolatry, there would be no rain in Israel (1 Kings 17:1). For the next three and a half years, Elijah prayed that God would shut the rain up in the heavens (see James 5:17).

The prophet's prayers were answered. During the years of drought that followed, Elijah lived by daily faith in the providence of God. In obedience to God's command, he went and hid in the Cherith Ravine, where he was fed every day by ravens (1 Kings 17:2–6). When the brook dried up, he went to Zarephath and trusted God for his daily bread there, too: day after day, the jar of flour was not used up and the jug of oil did not run dry, and thus there was fresh bread to eat every day (vv. 7–16). Elijah also had faith in God's resurrection power. When the young son of a widow died, the prophet prayed for his life to return, and the boy was saved (vv. 17–24).

Then Elijah went up on Mount Carmel to confront the prophets of Baal. Each side would prepare a sacrificial bull and pray to its deity. Whichever one answered by sending fire from heaven was the true God of Israel. Elijah let the prophets of Baal go first, giving them the "home-bull advantage." They prayed all day: "Come on, Baal, light my fire!" Nothing happened. But when Elijah prayed to the true and living God, fire came down from heaven and consumed everything (1 Kings 18:30–38). Nothing was left. No bull. No altar. No water. Then the people of Israel fell down and worshiped, while Elijah took the false prophets to the nearest river and put them to death (vv. 39–40).

Elijah was among the greatest of all the prophets—a spiritual giant. Frankly, he was the kind of person who had a lot to be humble about—more than most—and he *was* humble. First Kings 18 ends with him running ahead of King Ahab all the way to his palace in Jezreel (vv. 44–46). This is one of the great athletic feats of the Bible. In the power of the Holy Spirit, Elijah ran almost twenty miles and arrived before a horse and chariot. In doing this, the prophet humbly identified himself as a servant of the king, for in those days a king was preceded by heralds to announce the arrival of his royal person (see Est. 6:11).

In courage, faith, and humility, Elijah was a great man of God. He was probably the last person in Israel whom anyone expected to get so discouraged that he wanted to die. Yet as we read 1 Kings 19, we see many of the warning signs of suicide: Elijah wanted to die; he felt hopeless; he acted recklessly and slept excessively; and he felt isolated and withdrew from human companionship.[1] So what happened?

Suicidal Thoughts

When Ahab's chariot arrived at Jezreel, jealous Queen Jezebel was waiting to meet her king and hoping to hear good news. She heard instead that her prophets had been put to death, so she flew into a deadly rage and sent word to Elijah that he was next (1 Kings 19:2). Thus, Elijah learned that he was a dead man, and in that moment, all his courage abandoned him. The prophet's great faith was driven out by sudden anxiety. "Then he was afraid," Scripture says, "and he arose and ran for his life" (v. 3).

A man can run a long way when he is running for his life, and Elijah ran ninety miles, all the way to Beersheba. Then he went another day's journey into the desert (v. 4). He ran and ran until finally he threw himself down under a lonely tree. Then he prayed. After all, Elijah was a man of prayer. So how is this for a prayer? "It is enough; now, O LORD, take away my life, for I am no better than my fathers" (v. 4).

Notice that even at the point of absolute desperation—when he may have been the loneliest man in the world—Elijah still managed to pray. He took his complaint to God. Rather than taking his life, as he was tempted to do, he asked God if he could die. Deep down, the prophet knew that suicide is a sin—not an unforgivable sin, and often a sin of weakness rather than malice, but a sin nonetheless. So even when he wanted to die, Elijah acknowledged God's lordship over life and death. We see the same thing in Job (Job 10:18–19), Moses (Num. 11:15), Jeremiah (Jer. 20:14), and Jonah (Jonah 4:3). All of these men wished that they could die, but they did not kill themselves. Instead, they took their despair to God in prayer.

We see the same thing in the life of Jonathan Blanchard, the nineteenth-century abolitionist who served as the first president of Wheaton College. Blanchard was prone to bouts of despair, especially in the long winter months. One Sunday, he recorded in his journal that he felt "forsaken of God" and abandoned "in a state of torment, helpless." On Tuesday, he wrote that he continued to experience what he described as "a horror of darkness." Yet he also reported that he had turned to God in prayer, asking God to do for him what he could not do for himself.[2]

Anyone who has ever been depressed knows how Elijah felt. But even people who are never depressed can learn to be sensitive to the cries of anguish all around them. Elijah's desperate plea finds a modern echo in the 1996 film *Trainspotting*, in which the lead character says (edited for profanity):

> Choose life. Choose a job. Choose a career. Choose a family. Choose a big television. . . . Choose sitting on that couch watching mind-numbing, spirit-crushing game shows. . . . Choose rotting away at the end of it all . . . in a miserable home, nothing more than an embarrassment to the selfish . . . brats that you've spawned to replace yourselves. . . . But why would I want to do a thing like that? I chose not to choose life. I chose somethin' else. And the reasons? There are no reasons. Who needs reasons when you've got heroin?

Elijah never watched television or did drugs, but this is basically how he felt. By the time he reached that lonely tree in the wilderness, he was choosing not to choose life. Like the poet Donald Hall, he wanted to "sleep, rage, kill the day, and die."[3]

It is strange to say, but some people still have the idea that if they trust in Jesus, all their troubles will be over. God will get them better jobs, find them suitable mates, or remove temptations to sin. But salvation in Jesus Christ does not bring an end to life's troubles. In fact, sometimes they are just starting. Christians get hurt. We get discouraged and depressed. Sometimes we are so afraid that we abandon our calling and run for our lives, or face suicidal temptations. Even spiritual leaders get scared, quit, run away, and think about ending it all. So when we see Elijah lying under his tree, we also see our own weakness.

Spiritual Depression: Its Causes

It is not hard to come up with plausible explanations for Elijah's depression. He had at least half a dozen good reasons to be suicidal.

First, *fatigue*. Elijah was exhausted. He had run eighteen miles to Jezreel, then another ninety miles down to Beersheba. By the time he reached Mount Horeb, which is where his journey ended (1 Kings 19:8), he had run three hundred miles in all! As athletic as he was, Elijah was on the verge of complete physical collapse, and a tired believer is a vulnerable believer. As several great leaders are claimed to have said, fatigue makes cowards of us all.

Second, *isolation*. No Christian can thrive or survive without the communion of the saints. Yet Elijah had been virtually alone for more than three years. Now he was totally alone. Having deliberately left his servant behind in Beersheba (v. 3), Elijah had cut himself off from godly companionship.

Next, *spiritual opposition*. Elijah had stood all alone against all the prophets of Baal. He overcame them, but then he was opposed by Jezebel, that mistress of Satan. Thus, the prophet came under direct spiritual attack. Relentless spiritual opposition is bound to bring a believer to the point of despair.

Here is another explanation for Elijah's depression: *the normal rhythms of human emotion*. The prophet had just experienced a spiritual high, the ultimate mountaintop experience. He had witnessed the mighty acts of God in the fire on Mount Carmel. But then he came back down to earth, hard, and thus it is no surprise that he became a blue believer. No one can live a godly life on sheer emotion.

Add to Elijah's emotional fragility *the feeling of emptiness that often follows ministering in the name of God*. When Elijah was up on the mountain, the strength of the Lord surged through every molecule of his being. Now the vessel was empty. There is always something draining about serving as a conduit for the Word of God.

Maybe preachers understand Elijah's depression best of all. After they give everything to proclaiming the Word of God, often they are running on empty. Pastor Donald Baker describes this empty feeling in his book *Depression: Finding Hope and Meaning in Life's Darkest Shadow*:

> I could preach with fervor and power, I could share Christ with enthusiasm and success. I would counsel with meaningful insight and socialize with sheer delight. But without warning, any or all of these positive and delightful emotions would suddenly be forced to give way to feelings of gloom and periods of weakness. I would withdraw, and a form of paranoia would settle in. I would suddenly be overwhelmed with feelings of inadequacy and inferiority. On occasion I toyed with thoughts of self-destruction. . . . The struggle reached its inevitable climax when I found myself too weary to minister, too filled with hostility to love, and too frightened to preach.[4]

Then what about *dashed expectations*? Very likely Elijah went to the palace in Jezreel fully confident that he had won the day and that Israel would turn back to God. But meeting Queen Jezebel was a cold slap in the face. Although Elijah had won a battle, he had not yet won the war—a discouraging reality.

Along with Elijah's shattered expectations went the very

natural response of *fear*. Scripture is explicit about this: "Then he was afraid" (1 Kings 19:3). In that moment, when he was gripped with fear and his life passed before his very eyes, Elijah took his gaze off the Lord and fixed it squarely on his own troubles.

Then, on top of everything else, the prophet was dealing with *guilt*. Having run off in his own direction, Elijah was absent without leave. He had deserted his post in the middle of the battle, abandoning his divine calling at the very moment when the spiritual destiny of his nation was hanging in the balance. Thus, Elijah had failed miserably in the one area of life that was his greatest strength: bold faith. His self-condemnation was just: "I am no better than my fathers" (v. 4).

Many factors contributed to Elijah's spiritual depression. There are simple (or at least partial) remedies for most of them, and knowing these remedies is an important aspect of self-care. If we are struggling with spiritual depression, we should identify its causes as clearly as we can and apply the obvious practical remedy. So if we are tired, we should get some exercise and then get some rest. If our bodies are breaking down, we should eat healthy, balanced meals and, if necessary, receive proper medical care. If we are isolated, we should go to worship and speak with Christian friends. If we are under spiritual attack, we should pray for spiritual protection. If we are guilty, we should confess our sins to God and to one another.

Spiritual Depression: Its Cure

All of these remedies are fine as far as they go, but Elijah had a deeper need. When his story is fully and properly understood, it becomes apparent that he was crying out for a Savior—the Savior that we meet in Jesus Christ. When Elijah said that he was no better than his fathers, he was doing something more than confessing his sins; he was acknowledging that he was not the Prophet whom God had promised (see Deut. 18:15–18). Therefore, someone else would have to come and save God's people.

Eventually Elijah would meet the Savior for himself, with Moses on the Mount of Transfiguration (Matt. 17:1–13). But long before that day came, while Elijah was still under his lonely tree, God answered his prayers by showing him the same kind of grace that he gives to us in Jesus.

God did not abandon Elijah. In the darkest, loneliest moment of Elijah's life, God was right there with him. Scripture says that the prophet "lay down and slept under a broom tree. And behold, an angel touched him and said to him, 'Arise and eat.' And he looked, and behold, there was at his head a cake baked on hot stones and a jar of water. And he ate and drank and lay down again. And the angel of the LORD came again a second time and touched him and said, 'Arise and eat'" (1 Kings 19:5–7).

Elijah was touched by an angel—twice. The tenderness of this gesture makes it clear that God loved this man just as much under the broom tree, when he wanted to die, as he had loved him up on the mountaintop, when he was preaching the Word. Take this lesson to heart in every struggle: God could not love you any more than he does. His love for you in Jesus is not circumstantial; it is perpetual.

When Elijah had had enough, he discovered that God's grace is *more* than enough. In a time of deep discouragement, God sent an angel to touch his prophet with a gentle hand and speak to him in an audible voice. Then God gave Elijah the rest that he needed. He left his prophet to sleep safely and peacefully under the broom tree, and after he ate, to sleep again. Elijah's life-restoring nap fulfilled one of the Bible's most precious promises: the Lord "grants sleep to those he loves" (Ps. 127:2 NIV).

All of this is beautifully depicted in "Sleeping Elijah," a painting by the contemporary Chinese artist He Qi. In the painting, Elijah sleeps serenely on the ground while an angel hovers over him, overshadowing the sleeping prophet with soft wings and cupping one hand over his angelic mouth to whisper words of grace to him.

It was also God's grace to give Elijah fresh bread and cool water (and then, after his nap, to bring him seconds). God did all of this without one word of condemnation. Remember that Elijah had run away from his calling; therefore, he no longer had any legitimate claim on the blessing of God. But rather than turning his back on his prophet or telling him to stop feeling sorry for himself, God showed him grace upon grace. God wasn't finished with Elijah. His life still had a kingdom purpose. So does ours: no matter how discouraged we are today, God still has a bright plan for our tomorrow.

Admittedly, things did not get better for Elijah right away. In fact, they got worse. The prophet traveled forty days and forty nights to Horeb, the mountain of God. By the end of those forty days, he was as discouraged as ever, which is not surprising. Depression can be hard to shake. Getting rid of it requires more than taking two Bible verses and calling your pastor in the morning. Even the strongest Christians may need months to return to joyful service in the kingdom of God.

When Elijah reached the mountain, he went into a cave (probably the cave where God had long ago appeared to Moses; see Ex. 33:20–23) and held his own private pity party. "I have been very jealous for the LORD, the God of hosts," he said. "For the people of Israel have forsaken your covenant, thrown down your altars, and killed your prophets with the sword, and I, even I only, am left, and they seek my life, to take it away" (1 Kings 19:10).

This was not Elijah's finest moment. The prophet's speech was riddled with half-truths, partial falsehoods, and careless exaggerations that made his situation seem much worse than it actually was—a common temptation for people who are feeling depressed. The repetition of his words in verse 14 suggests that he had been rehearsing this speech all the way to Mount Horeb. Elijah was full of self-righteousness, self-importance, and self-pity. "Poor me," he was saying. The undeniable fact is that he had run away from his calling. Yet all that he could think about was everything that he had done for God—and everything that God wasn't doing for him.

What we say to ourselves is very important. When we are depressed, it is tempting to say things like "I deserve better than this"; "I can't take it anymore"; "No one can help me"; "No one can solve my problems"; "Nobody loves me"; "Nobody cares"; or "I am the only one." If this is what we tell ourselves, then it is no wonder that we are discouraged! Instead, we need to preach the gospel to ourselves, reminding ourselves that because we are accepted in Christ, God will never leave us or forsake us.

God did not abandon Elijah at Horeb. He was still there

for him. He continued to have compassion on his prophet. He spoke to him again—not in the wind, earthquake, or fire, but in a "still small voice" (1 Kings 19:12 KJV). And when God spoke, he gently called Elijah back into active service for his kingdom (vv. 15–18).

By the mercy of God, Elijah's faithful ministry as a prophet continued to bless the people of God. Far from ending his ministry, Elijah's season of depression laid the foundation for further fruitfulness. Charles Spurgeon testified to a similar grace in his life:

> I often feel very grateful to God that I have undergone fearful depression of spirits. I know the borders of despair, and the horrible brink of that gulf of darkness into which my feet have almost gone; but hundreds of times I have been able to give a helpful grip to brethren and sisters who have come into that same condition, which grip I could never have given if I had not known their deep despondency. So I believe that the darkest and most dreadful experience of a child of God will help him to be a fisher of men if he will but follow Christ.[5]

The way God cared for Elijah at Mount Horeb and under the broom tree helps us understand how to help people who are discouraged or depressed. They may not need very much advice. They probably don't need us to tell them what's wrong with them. They may not need anyone to say very much at all. But they do need a gentle touch, the ministry of our personal presence, and someone to help care for their daily needs. They also need to know that they are deeply loved—not only by us, but also by the God who still has a loving purpose for their lives.

One dark night, one of my children was in real distress—a distress that was mainly of her own making. I asked myself: "What does this child need? A strong word of correction? The threat of discipline? A word of encouragement?"

Depending on the circumstances, any one of these responses might be appropriate. But what my daughter needed that night is what most people need most of the time. She needed a gentle hand on her shoulder. She needed to hear again that she was deeply and truly loved. And she needed to know that she was not stuck in her sadness; there was hope for her future.

You are a child of God, and therefore, your heavenly Father has the same grace for you. He will give you everything that he gave to Elijah. And he will give it to you in Jesus Christ, who is God's rest for the weary soul. Jesus says, "Come to me, all who labor and are heavy laden, and I will give you rest" (Matt. 11:28). Jesus is also daily bread and living water. So he says, "I am the bread of life; whoever comes to me shall not hunger, and whoever believes in me shall never thirst" (John 6:35). Jesus Christ is forgiveness for sin; there is no condemnation for anyone who trusts in him—not now, not ever (Rom. 8:1).

More than Enough

Whenever we feel as if we have had enough, we need to go back to Jesus and learn again that he is more than enough. This is not simply a Sunday school answer, it's the complete answer, because Jesus is everything we need. Jesus hears the prayers of anguish that we offer in our solitary places. He knows our discouragement and our depression, if that's how bad things are. He hears our cries for help and does not abandon us. He still loves us and is reaching out to touch us. He wants to forgive our ungodly sins and grant rest to our weary souls.

In response to what she was learning about God's grace for her in times of trouble, one Wheaton College student wrote the following creed—"A Creed for Myself," as she called it:

> I believe in grace. Not just the once-and-for-all kind that went to work while Jesus was on the cross, but grace that daily infiltrates my life, that offers me forgiveness when I inevitably sin, that offers me present and future redemption. . . . I believe.
>
> There is more than just this believing. There is deep pain here too. There is an exile that seems to resurrect more often than my joy, and a weariness right now that I can't even understand. I could fill up pages with the turmoil inside of me. But for now, it is enough to say this. To wrestle and to weep and to choose to claim within my heart that in and through everything, I still believe.[6]

Faith rises in our hearts every time we go back to Jesus and the cross, which is where the story of Elijah's desperate depression should point us.

Back in the nineteenth century, the German preacher F. W. Krummacher eloquently compared Elijah's tree to the cross where Jesus died. His words serve both as a fitting conclusion to the prophet's story and as a wise encouragement for our own pilgrimage:

> Listen. As often as it will seem to you as if it were enough, as if the burden of life is no longer to be borne, do as Elijah did. Flee you, too, to the silence of solitude, and I will show

you a [tree], and there you will cast yourself down. It is the cross. Yes, a [tree], covered with thorns and barbs that pierce the soul, girded about with . . . nails that wound the heart and cause . . . pain and suffering. But this [tree] also has a scent that refreshes the soul. . . . In the presence of the cross you no longer think of complaining about the greatness of your sufferings. For . . . the love of God in Jesus Christ for you poor sinner will soon draw all your thoughts and reflections away from everything else. . . . Under the cross your complaining will soon be absorbed in the peace of the Lord.[7]

"Where You Die I Will Die"

Ruth's Grief and Poverty

(Ruth 1:1–18)

In the days of the judges—when there was no king in Israel and there had been famine in the land—Ruth was in trouble. Real trouble. After a season of prosperity, her family had suffered one disaster after another: hunger, poverty, and the death of every adult male who could protect and provide. As she stood partway down the long, dusty road that led from Moab to Bethlehem, Ruth had a choice to make—a choice that would determine her destiny and play a small but indispensable part in the big story of our salvation.

The Problems Ruth Faced

To understand how much trouble Ruth was in, as well as the saving consequences of her choice, we need to enter her world.

Who was Ruth, what was her experience, and what help did she find in her time of trouble?

In the providence of God, Ruth had married a man from Bethlehem. This in itself was somewhat unusual, for Ruth was not a Jew, but a Moabite, and in those days, most Jewish men did not take foreign brides. The Moabites specifically were forbidden to worship in the assembly of Israel (Deut. 23:3). Nevertheless, Ruth had married Mahlon, whose family had fled to the country of Moab in order to escape a desperate famine in Israel. For nearly a decade, they lived in peace and prosperity. There were five of them altogether: Ruth and Mahlon, his mother Naomi (who was a widow, her husband having died after they arrived in Moab), and his brother Chilion, who was married to Orpah, another Moabite.

Then everything changed. In short order, Mahlon and Chilion also died. We do not know the cause of death, but we do know the result: Naomi, Ruth, and Orpah were on their own in a culture that gave every privilege to men. Thus, these women were in all kinds of trouble.

To begin with, they were grieving the loss of their husbands, which is one of the most painful sorrows that anyone can suffer. On the Holmes-Rahe Stress Inventory, "Death of Spouse" is number one on the list, and nothing else comes close. No matter when it happens—whether a couple is young or old—the death of a husband or wife changes everything. The grieving process takes years and the effects last for a lifetime. As one woman said: "When I lost my husband, I lost my best friend. . . . I lost my life's companion. . . . I lost my confidante. . . . I lost my dream of the future. . . . I lost my business partner. . . . I lost part of myself."[1]

Maybe Ruth felt the same way, as if she had lost part of herself. Our hearts go out to her as a grieving widow. Ruth's suffering reminds us of our own sad losses and the sorrows of people we love. Everyone carries a burden. It could be the death of a father or mother, brother or sister—something we think about every day. It could be the death of a dream—something we hoped would happen, but now we know never will. It could be the death of the family we thought we had, but now everything has come undone. Grief is the pain of knowing life will never be the same.

But that is not all. The death of three men from one family had devastating social and financial implications. Tell this story to anyone from the ancient world and ask them what would happen next, and they would say that these women were facing destitution and danger. Soon Naomi would be homeless in Bethlehem. Ruth was hard up against it, too. Without any land to call her own, and without any source of income, she would be reduced to living as an immigrant and gathering something to eat from the edge of someone's field. These women would have to be careful where they went, too, because men would try to take advantage of them. The last chapters of Judges tell a sordid tale of sexual violence in that era: rape, murder, and dismemberment.

Perhaps few of the people reading this book have ever been poor enough to understand the troubles that these women faced. But if we have been more fortunate, we should pause to lament the sorrows of a hurting world. Today there are perhaps a billion women who can relate all too well to this biblical narrative. There are millions of widows like Naomi and poor young women like Ruth. They are living in slums, begging on the streets, trapped in the sex trade, or traveling as refugees from one country to the next.

Is there room in your heart for the poor and the broken? Is there space in your life for women and children in danger? Do you do anything to help immigrants and refugees?

As we consider a world in need, perhaps we can relate to this prayer from South Africa, as shared by Archbishop Desmond Tutu:

> God, my Father
> I am filled
> With anguish and puzzlement.
> Why, oh God, is there so much
> Suffering, such needless suffering?
> Everywhere we look there is pain
> And suffering. . . .
> Why must there be so much killing,
> So much death and destruction,
> So much bloodshed,
> So much suffering,
> So much oppression, and injustice, and poverty
> and hunger?

Tutu's prayer does not end with a question, but with a cautiously hopeful answer that is based on the gospel:

> This is the world
> You loved so much that for it
> You gave your only begotten
> Son, our Lord and Saviour Jesus Christ, to hang
> From the cross, done to death
> Love nearly overwhelmed by hate

Light nearly extinguished by darkness
Life nearly destroyed by death—
But not quite—[2]

Every year, students in the Human Needs and Global Re-
sources program at Wheaton College offer a similar prayer: "In
a world of violence between persons, clans, and nations; of violence upon the self; where families are fractured through broken
relationships, . . . and where hatred and war are common to the
news . . . in such a world, God, what do you want us to do?"

As the liturgy continues, this prayer for guidance receives a
clear answer: "We are called, simply, to hold on to Christ and his
cross with one hand, with all our might; and to hold on to those
we are called to love with the other hand, with all our might,
with courage, humor, self-abandonment, creativity, flair, tears,
silence, sympathy, gentleness, flexibility, Christ-Likeness."[3]

The Choice Ruth Made

When it comes to holding on to Christ with one hand and people
we love with the other, it would be hard to find a better example
than Ruth, who made a life-or-death commitment to stay with
Naomi.

Picture the scene and feel its dramatic tension. Three women
were standing on the horizon, heading out into the wilderness.
Before they got anywhere close to Bethlehem, Naomi stopped
in the middle of the road and told her daughters-in-law to turn
around and go back home to Moab. She blessed them for their
kindness, but she also told them in no uncertain terms that they
should go home, where hopefully they could find other men to
marry.

At this point, both young women burst into tears. The scene is about as close as the Bible gets to a soap opera. Ruth and Orpah "lifted up their voices and wept" (Ruth 1:9). They said to Naomi, "No, we will return with you to your people" (v. 10). But Naomi would have none of it. She had no hope for a husband, and thus could offer no guarantee of provision or protection—a bitter truth that cut the old widow to the heart. "No, my daughters," she said, "it is exceedingly bitter to me for your sake that the hand of the LORD has gone out against me" (v. 13).

Naomi's anguish touched off another round of tears; all three women "lifted up their voices and wept again" (v. 14). They were wailing as women do in the Middle East. When they finally dried their tears, Orpah made the sensible choice. She loved Naomi well enough to walk part of the way to Bethlehem, but imagining that she would be better off back home, she kissed Naomi good-bye. Who could possibly blame her?

Ruth made the opposite choice, though, with massive consequences. What she decided would lead to the salvation of the world. See what she did: while Orpah was saying her last good-byes, Ruth was clinging to Naomi. Here the Bible uses an intensive verb to indicate an unbreakable bond. We can imagine Ruth hugging Naomi, and then, as her mother-in-law began to walk away, clutching her robes to prevent her from leaving without her. Ruth simply refused to let go.

At first, Naomi tried to push her away. "See," she said, "your sister-in-law has gone back to her people and to her gods; return after your sister-in-law" (v. 15). These words clarified what was at stake spiritually. The choice that confronted Ruth and Orpah was not merely about geographic location, ethnic identity, or the relative odds of finding a life partner in one community or the other. No, in the midst of trouble, these women were choosing whether they wanted to follow the true and living God.

Ruth had already made her choice. She was so resolute that once Naomi heard what her daughter-in-law had to say, she realized that it was pointless to argue. Ruth said: "Do not urge me to leave you or to return from following you. For where you go I will go, and where you lodge I will lodge. Your people shall be my people, and your God my God. Where you die I will die, and there will I be buried. May the LORD do so to me and more also if anything but death parts me from you" (vv. 16–17).

Word for word, this may be the best speech that anyone has ever given. It is a confession of faith from a woman of faith. In the clearest, strongest possible terms, Ruth tells the world what it means to belong to God and to his people. When trouble came, the woman did not give up, but doubled down. She made a life-or-death commitment to the God of Israel.

This is not the choice that most people make when they are in this much trouble. Instead of going with God, most people blame him for all their troubles, as Naomi did. Consider the testimony of Rose Thurgood, who was born in 1602 and wrote a personal narrative about her spiritual experience. Here is what Thurgood wrote about her spiritual response to a terrible illness that struck her family:

> And thus we lay very sick a month, and my children were sometimes so hot in their fits, that none could quench their drought, and fainted away. . . . And I now seeing myself in this extreme poverty and want and all my household was sick again, and withal the Lord gave me over to hardness of

heart again, then I began to rage and swell at God himself, saying to myself, what a God is this, what doth he mind to do with my children, surely they will die. And thus I began to quarrel with God.[4]

Naomi said more or less the same thing: "What kind of God is this, and what does he think he is doing to my family?" But Ruth made a different choice. When trouble came, she chose to go with God, even when her sister-in-law was going in the opposite direction. It was the choice to embark on a long and dangerous journey that no woman should take alone. It was the choice of a new cultural identity in a world where this was almost inconceivable. It was also the choice to stay with her mother-in-law, which at the very most was a mixed blessing: Naomi was so bitter that when she arrived in Bethlehem, people hardly recognized her.

There were lots of disincentives for Ruth to go with God. There always are! When it comes to the big choices in life—the choices that determine one's spiritual destiny—there are always all kinds of reasons to do something else. If Ruth went to Bethlehem, she was choosing to go down a dangerous road, with a difficult person, to an unfamiliar destination. But rather than giving up on God, she made the right choice, the best choice, and what for her was the only choice. Ruth wanted to be "all in" with the living God. As far as she was concerned, this was not a gamble, but a certainty by faith. So with God himself as her witness, she made a solemn vow to follow him to the very death.

One of the things that inspires me the most about Ruth is that she made her choice when she was young, probably still in her twenties. But at any age, the decisions we make today chart a course for eternity. No matter who we are or what has happened—whether everything is going right for us or desperately wrong—we have the rest of life ahead of us.

If we are wise, we will go with God, wherever he calls us to go. Some believers serve in the business world, where there are opportunities to create value for people made in God's image. Others serve in education and teach people about the world that God has made. Artists display truth and beauty with the sights and sounds of creation. Other Christians have callings in science, medicine, law, or public policy. Many others are still figuring out what to do and where to go, in which case the most important thing to do right away is to tell God—without any reservation—that we are willing to go wherever he wants us to go. If we go with God, he will give us the opportunity to do something useful for the kingdom.

If we are wise, we will also stay with God, wherever he calls us to stay. We should never underestimate how hard this can be. Sometimes staying with God is a lot harder than going with God. Everything inside us is crying out to do a different job, in a different place, with different people. But if that is not God's path for us, then it is not the right path, no matter how much easier it would be. Stay with God and with his people. Wherever we go in the world, we should hold on to the church the way Ruth held on to Naomi. The only way to stay with God in the world is to stay close to his people.

Go with God, stay with God. Live with God, die with God, and then live with him forever. This was Ruth's choice, and it became her destiny. It will be our destiny, too, if we choose for God the way Ruth did.

The Consequences of Ruth's Choice

What were the consequences of Ruth's choice? Some people say it's not the destination that matters, only the journey. But when it comes to the life of the human soul, it is the destination that makes the journey worthwhile. So we need to know the rest of the story. What happened to Ruth and to her mother-in-law, Naomi?

To begin with, their relationship was a mutual blessing. Naomi had the support of Ruth's encouragement and companionship, and vice versa. Therefore, these women enjoyed what Francis Bacon described as the "two contrary effects" of human friendship: "it redoubles joys and cuts griefs in half."[5] Ruth and Naomi also had the kind of relationship that Aelred of Rievaulx wrote about in his classic treatise *On Spiritual Friendship*.[6] Aelred was the leader of a monastic community in Yorkshire, England, during the twelfth century. He wanted to help unmarried Christians experience life-changing community through loving relationships. So he contrasted "carnal friendship," which is based merely on the shared pursuit of pleasure, and "worldly friendship," which is based on mutual advantage, with "spiritual friendship," which is grounded in shared discipleship. The carnal friend says, "Let's party!" The worldly friend says, "If you scratch my back, I'll scratch yours." But the true spiritual friend says, "Let's help each other follow Jesus" (which, by the way, gives the most real joy and yields the best genuine advantages in life).

Aelred's categories give us a good way to test the quality of our relationships: Am I in this friendship because it makes me feel good—because of what I can get out of it—or because this friendship is helping me grow in godliness?

Ruth was a true spiritual friend to Naomi. These women were almost alone in the world, but they did have each other, and they were walking together down the path where they would find God's presence and flourish under his provision. From the moment when Ruth made her choice to go with God, and also with Naomi and the people of God, she experienced one blessing after another. This is what happens to people who go with God when they get into trouble: they get the help they need.

Ruth and Naomi arrived in Bethlehem just as the barley harvest was beginning—a sign of God's provision. The next day, Ruth went out to glean some grain from the edge of a nearby field. This is how poor people survived in those days; it was the biblical form of "workfare."

In the providence of God, Ruth just so happened to end up in the field of Boaz—a godly man who protected the women who came to his fields from any kind of abuse (see Ruth 2:8–9). That night, Ruth came home with a shawl full of barley. Naomi was excited about this, not simply because the women had enough to eat, but also because she realized that Boaz was a close enough relative to fulfill the sacred obligation to marry Ruth, produce an heir, and rescue the entire family from poverty. To use the biblical term for it, Boaz was eligible to serve as their kinsman-redeemer.

Naomi acted quickly. She told Ruth to wear her best outfit, put on sweet perfume, and approach Boaz with a proposal of marriage. That night, Ruth seized her chance and boldly claimed the most eligible bachelor in Bethlehem. This romance became her redemption. The next day, Boaz got a license from the city elders, the happy couple married, and nine months later, Naomi was holding a grandson in her lap. So a story that began with three funerals ended with a wedding and a baby shower.

It wasn't just any baby, either. The boy was named Obed. He became the father of Jesse and therefore the grandfather of David, who started the world's one and only eternal dynasty: the kingdom of David's son, Jesus Christ. Thus, Ruth's choice was an indispensable part of the story of our salvation. Ray Bakke summarizes her story like this: "Ruth, a Moabite and a descendant of Sodom, is choreographed into the early history of Israel by becoming the great-grandmother of Israel's greatest king and an ancestor of Jesus on his earthly side."[7] No Ruth, no Obed. No Obed, no Jesse. No Jesse, no David. No David, no Savior born to us in the City of David, and therefore no salvation.

Happily Ever After

Praise God for the choice that Ruth made! When trouble came, she did not give up on God or turn her back on him, but redoubled her commitment to him and rededicated her life to following him, no matter what. And when she did, she found the help that she needed: comfort for sorrow, food in a time of famine, refuge under God's wings (see Ruth 2:12), and love from his people, with heaps of romance thrown in for good measure.

This is the way all the really good stories go: from death and despair to happily ever after. So do not take the easy way out; make the hard choice instead. When the situation is desperate and even God seems to be going against you, do not give up, but trust his good plan. Believe, as Ruth did, that the words of the prophet are true: "The LORD is good, a stronghold in the day of trouble" (Nah. 1:7).

Earlier in this chapter, I shared part of the story of Rose Thurgood, a Christian woman from the seventeenth century. When Rose's family fell sick, she despaired of life itself. But in her time of trouble, God reminded her that he was with her. In her autobiography, Thurgood wrote, "I felt a sweet flash coming over my heart and suddenly these words were pronounced in my heart: Thy name is written in the book of life."[8]

Ruth's name is written in the same place, and so is your name, by the grace that God has for you in Jesus Christ. The best stories are full of trouble, which starts in the early chapters and always gets worse before it gets better. But all's well that ends well. So when trouble comes, go with Jesus and stay with Jesus all the way to eternal life.

4

"You Are the Man!"

David's Deadly Temptation
(2 Samuel 11:1–5; 12:1–15)

It was in the springtime—the season of the year when kings go out to battle—and David was in trouble. Real trouble. Late one afternoon, as he strolled around the rooftop of his palace in Jerusalem, his eye chanced upon the form of a beautiful woman. At that moment, he did not intend to commit a scandalous sin. Yet he was about to give in to a passionate temptation that would bring his household to grief.

Untouchable

If you had watched David's rise to power, you never would have expected him to become a murderer or an adulterer. He was the kind of man whom mothers hope their daughters will marry and fathers wish they could have for a son.

David was called by God. When he was still a boy, the prophet Samuel visited David's house—a divine appointment. His older brothers looked more impressive, but the Lord looks at the heart, and according to his divine plan, the youngest son was the chosen one. So Samuel anointed David to be king over Israel.

David was strengthened by faith. When Goliath defied the armies of Israel and mocked the name of the living God, David went out to meet him in battle. Armed only with a slingshot and a few choice stones, the boy took dead aim and slew the mighty giant. His victory did not come by superior strength or skill, but by absolute trust in the power of God. Before he went into battle, David said, "The LORD who delivered me from the paw of the lion and from the paw of the bear will deliver me from the hand of this Philistine" (1 Sam. 17:37).

David was patient in waiting. In the long years between his anointing and his coronation—when Saul was on the throne and David wasn't—he did not claim the kingdom for himself, but waited for God to give it to him. Even when Saul tried to kill him, David did not retaliate, but trusted God to put him on the throne when the time was right.

David was easy to love. His very name means "Beloved." King Saul loved him, at least at first. Saul's son Jonathan loved him, too, even though it would cost him his father's kingdom. Jonathan's sister Michal also loved David. In fact, she is the first and maybe the only woman in the Bible who is said in so many words to love a man (1 Sam. 18:20). Soldiers loved

David so much that they risked their lives for him. The people of Israel loved David and sang his praises. Most important, the Lord loved David, for the Bible calls him "a man after [God's] own heart" (1 Sam. 13:14).

David was exuberant with praise. The king was a poet—the sweet singer of Israel. His lyrical ballads became the songs that people sang when they worshiped God in his holy temple. "The LORD is my shepherd," David wrote (Ps. 23:1); "I will bless the LORD at all times; his praise shall continually be in my mouth" (34:1); "I will give thanks to the LORD with my whole heart" (9:1); and "I will sing praise to the name of the LORD, the Most High" (7:17).

Surely a man like David would be safe from any danger! Has anyone ever offered more praise to God or expressed stronger confidence in his saving power? If David had continued to walk with God, he would have been blessed even more. He would have become the king of an everlasting kingdom. Nonetheless, David was in trouble. A man can be called by God and loved by God, yet still come under sudden attack. A man can trust in God, wait for God, fight for God, sing praise to God, and still give in to a deadly temptation. If it happened to someone as untouchable as David, it could happen to anyone.

Christians today are as blessed as David was, if not more so. We are loved by our Father God. We have the gift of faith by the work of the Holy Spirit. We have been called by Jesus Christ into the service of his kingdom. We gather frequently for worship with the people of God. It would be easy to assume, therefore, that we are totally safe.

But we are not safe—we're in constant danger. Scripture

says, "Let anyone who thinks that he stands take heed lest he fall" (1 Cor. 10:12). Our enemy constantly looks for an opportunity to destroy us, and the times when we think we are totally safe may be the times of greatest danger.

What temptation will you face today? We are all tempted. As Thomas à Kempis once said, "There is no man that is altogether free from temptations while he liveth on earth: for in ourselves is the root thereof."[1] The question is: are we ready to face temptation, or are we in as much trouble as David was late one afternoon when he decided to go out and take a walk on the roof of his royal palace?

A Royal Omission

Before we see what David did wrong and what happened afterward, we should notice what David *didn't* do. Sometimes when we are struggling with a particular sin, we focus on *not* doing something: not binging on food, for example, or not criticizing people we find hard to love, or not indulging some impure pleasure. And, of course, there is a place for not doing things that are not pleasing to God. After all, the Bible does say, on occasion, "Thou shalt not . . ."

What first got David in trouble, however, was not something that he did; it was something that he *didn't* do: "In the spring of the year, the time when kings go out to battle, David sent Joab, and his servants with him, and all Israel" (2 Sam. 11:1a). The Bible never wastes a detail, and these particular details are an indictment. Kings were supposed to go out and do battle. So by retreating to his palace, David was failing to do his royal duty. He had stopped serving or sacrificing his life for others. The fact that he was sitting on the couch at the beginning of this story says it all. But in case there is any doubt about this, the Bible reiterates: "David remained at Jerusalem" (v. 1b). The repetition is for emphasis. The king should have led his troops into battle; instead, he sent them into harm's way.

Apparently David's success had made him lazy. He had a sense of entitlement. He wanted to enjoy his luxuries, and thus he couldn't be bothered with the hard work of defending his kingdom. Is it really a surprise that David's self-indulgence led him into greater transgression?

We should be careful not to miss the opportunity to examine our own lives: What am I *not* doing that I should do, and how might that failure lead me to do things I never planned to do and don't even want to do? Some of the things that people don't do are very familiar, so they are easy to overlook. But if we are not doing them, then we are already in more trouble than we realize.

Here are a few simple questions to ask about what we are—and are not—doing:

Have I been in conversation with God today, or is prayer one of those things that I am not doing as much as I should? Jesus told his disciples to watch and pray so that they would not fall into temptation (Matt. 26:41). If we fail to watch and pray, how can we expect to stay out of the kind of trouble that David got into? One old Puritan wisely prayed: "Teach me to believe that if I would ever have any sin subdued I must not only labor to overcome it, but must invite Christ to abide in the place of it, and he must become more to me than that vile lust had been; that his sweetness, power, life may be there."[2]

Here is another simple question: *Am I feeding on the Word*

of God? I use the word *feeding* because we need to do something more than simply read our Bibles. We need to draw daily nourishment from Scripture, so that we remember God's promises and know what he is calling us to do in the world.

Or consider this question: *Am I actively engaged in the worship of God, especially in the life of a local church?* The Holy Spirit calls us to be present in worship—not just occupying space, but giving mind, heart, and soul to the honor and majesty of our Savior.

We also have work to do. God has given each of us a main calling in life. *Am I dedicating my very best to him? Or is something else getting in the way—social media, perhaps, or a hobby that takes more of my time than it should?* If we let things that are permissible get in the way of what is vital, we will end up like King David: getting into trouble because we're not doing what we ought to be doing when and where we are supposed to be doing it.

What David Did

Understand that sexual sin is never just about sex; it is always connected to the rest of life. If David had been living for others instead of for himself—if he had been living sacrificially rather than self-indulgently—maybe he could have kept his desire under the power of love. But that is not how David was living.

Then he caught a glimpse of a beautiful woman. If that is all that he had done, he still would not have been guilty of any sin. But David did more than catch a glimpse. His glance became a gaze. He looked her up and down, thinking about what he'd like to do with her sexually.

From this point on, the story unfolds like a slow-motion replay of a train wreck. We have seen it before and we can hardly bear to look again, but we watch it anyway, hoping for a different ending. But, of course, it turns out the same way every time. If only David had turned away!

In the anatomy of temptation, the eye is a window to the heart. Therefore, one way to gain victory over sexual sin is to turn away our lusty gaze. Godly men and women have always understood that such victory requires modesty in the way we dress, the way we speak, and what we choose to keep looking at. The apostle Peter wisely warned against having "eyes full of adultery" (2 Pet. 2:14). Job's remedy for lust-free living was a proactive promise: "I made a covenant with my eyes not to look lustfully at a girl" (Job 31:1 NIV).

Being careful what we see has never been more important than it is today, when there are sexual images everywhere we look. North Americans are living in a "pornotopia," where porn has become the norm. Pornography puts us all in danger. It denigrates women and men, damages relationships, and destroys our spiritual ability to lead. The Puritan Thomas Watson rightly said that sexual pictures "secretly convey poison to the heart."[3] Pornography also affects the brain in dramatic ways, as Bill Struthers has documented in his book *Wired for Intimacy*.[4] A person who succumbs to pornography deteriorates spiritually. Giving in to sexual temptation produces what John Freeman aptly calls a "pornified heart"—a heart that is no longer fully available to God or to other people. Writing specifically to men, Freeman warns: "Our sexual sins not only cause our hearts to go dead, but they also keep us from being who and what we should be as men, husbands, and fathers. Due to years of sexual temptations, and unforsaken sins, our neglected hearts will rob everyone in our lives of something!"[5]

To see how deadly lust is, we need only see what happened to David. The longer he looked at the woman, the more he wanted her. Sin was taking control, and as David began to fantasize, he felt unable to turn away. Rather than fleeing from temptation—like Joseph did, when Potiphar's beautiful wife grabbed him and wanted to have sex with him (Gen. 39:12)—David began to do what the Bible tells us not to do: he began to "think about how to gratify the desires of the sinful nature" (Rom. 13:14 NIV).

David didn't have to do this. In fact, the Bible gives us this amazing promise: "God is faithful, and he will not let you be tempted beyond your ability, but with the temptation he will also provide the way of escape, that you may be able to endure it" (1 Cor. 10:13). If we doubt this promise, it is probably because we have never really tested it. Usually, we give in to temptation much too soon, and thus we fail to find the exit strategy that God has for us. But a way of escape is always there. God has a promise for us to claim, a friend for us to call, and a living Holy Spirit to come and help us when we pray. The next time you are tempted to commit the sin that keeps dragging you down, try this. Pray out loud: "Lord Jesus, I am tempted to this sin against you. Show me the way out!"

When we pray this way, our prayers will be answered. Freeman notes that real spiritual change "isn't measured just by what we stop doing. It's always measured in character change." And when it comes to sexual sanctification, the changes will be dramatic: "Whereas your former preoccupation with yourself robbed others, now you begin to be more interested in others than yourself. You see yourself wanting to bless others, desiring their good and not just your own. You no longer hide what you are doing; instead, you are increasingly open with others about your struggles and faults."[6]

Sadly, instead of looking for God's escape and living with greater openness, King David started toying with sin. That is what lust is: looking at a man or a woman and imagining the sexual possibilities. In this case, "the woman was very beautiful, and David sent someone to find out about her. The man said, 'Isn't this Bathsheba, the daughter of Eliam and the wife of Uriah the Hittite?'" (2 Sam. 11:3 NIV). Obviously, the whole affair should have ended right there. "The double identification," writes David Wolpe, "reinforces how much she cannot belong to David. She is a woman with both a husband and a father. She is under the care and protection of others. Hands off."[7]

Giving Bathsheba any further thought was out of the question for a man of God, but David wanted to have her. This is the way lust works. It takes on a life of its own, pulling us in deeper and deeper until we feel powerless to resist. And since David was the king, he could do what most men can only dream of doing. If he wanted a woman, he could have her, and so he fetched Bathsheba: "She came to him, and he lay with her" (v. 4).

It seemed like such a small thing—only a moment of weakness, nothing more. But soon Bathsheba discovered that she was pregnant, and the cover-up began. One thing led to another, and by the time David was finished summoning noble Uriah back to Jerusalem, getting him drunk, and then sending him back to the army with orders that amounted to a death sentence, it was more than a sex scandal. Bathsheba's husband was dead and David had become a felon. He was guilty of adultery, deceit, theft, and murder: the cover-up was much worse than the crime.

For a while, it seemed as if David would get away with murder. One commentator imagines him feeling the "slightly-uneasy-but-exhilarated sense of a man who has sinned and gotten away with it."[8] Most of us know the feeling. Sure, the king had to scramble a little bit to make it happen, but everything went according to plan. Except for this: "The thing that David had done displeased the LORD" (v. 27).

If we are trying to cover up a sin, we should not imagine that God does not know what we have done. Concealing any sin is futile in the sight of an all-knowing God. If we have done something to displease him, we may be sure that he knows all about it. Solomon stated this principle explicitly in the context of sexual sin: "Why should you be intoxicated, my son, with a forbidden woman and embrace the bosom of an adulteress? For a man's ways are before the eyes of the LORD, and he ponders all his paths" (Prov. 5:20–21).

David's Confession

So what should David have done? When trouble first came, in the form of a deadly temptation, he gave right in. This got him into a lot more trouble. Deep down, he must have known this. There seemed to be no way out. So what should he have done?

If anyone knew what to do in times of trouble, it was David, who had been in trouble many times before. And whenever he had found himself in trouble, David had known what to do: pray for God to deliver him. We see this again and again in the

Psalms. "Be not far from me," David prayed, "for trouble is near, and there is none to help (Ps. 22:11); "The troubles of my heart are enlarged; bring me out of my distresses" (25:17). Yet this time, we hear nothing from the man—nothing, that is, until God had mercy on him and sent him a true spiritual friend.

Thank God, David had someone in his life who cared enough to confront him. We live in a culture that believes love means never having to tell anyone that he or she is wrong. But this is not what Nathan the prophet believed, at all. He loved King David well enough to tell him that he was a sinner.

It was clever how Nathan did it, too. It was like spiritual judo. The prophet used the weight of David's own opinion against him and persuaded the king to render judgment before he knew the identity of the accused. Nathan did this by telling a parable of injustice, in which a wealthy stockholder stole a poor man's only lamb and served it for dinner. Somehow the story reoriented David's moral compass. It penetrated his defenses and captured his conscience. As a righteous king, he was ready to put the rich man to death right away. David's indignation proved to be the perfect setup for Nathan's signature line. "You are the man!" he said (2 Sam. 12:7).

Then the prophet outlined David's transgressions in painful detail. God had anointed David as king. He had rescued his life from his enemies and established his kingdom. He had given him houses and lands, with women to spare. Yet David had slept with another man's wife and then struck the good man down in cold blood. By doing this, he had "utterly scorned the LORD" (v. 14), and as a result, his home would become a place of strife and scandal.

79

David was in disgrace, but there was one thing he did right—the only thing he did right in this entire story—and that was to confess his sin. "You're right, Nathan," he said. "I am the man." Or, as the Bible quotes him, "I have sinned against the LORD" (v. 13).

We get David's full confession in Psalm 51—a song of painful beauty. David did not make any more excuses. He was done trying to pretend that God did not know what he had done. He saw his sin for what it was, and he was man enough to admit it:

Have mercy on me, O God,
according to your steadfast love;
according to your abundant mercy
blot out my transgressions.
Wash me thoroughly from my iniquity,
and cleanse me from my sin!
For I know my transgressions,
and my sin is ever before me.
Against you, you only, have I sinned
and done what is evil in your sight,
so that you may be justified in your words
and blameless in your judgment. (Ps. 51:1–4)

God always has mercy on people who confess their sins. So God took away David's sin (see 2 Sam. 12:13). He renewed David's hope. He restored David's faith. He created a clean heart in him and renewed his spirit. In fact, by the time David got to the end of Psalm 51, he was ready to lead God's people in worship. "O Lord," he prayed, "open my lips, and my mouth will declare your praise" (Ps. 51:15).

More than anyone else in the Bible, King David declared that

God delivers people who are in trouble. "The salvation of the righteous is from the LORD," he testified; "he is their stronghold in the time of trouble" (Ps. 37:39).

Some people find it hard to believe this promise because some particular sin seems to dominate their lives. But anyone who feels powerless is actually in the perfect place to see God do something that could never happen any other way. Our own attempts at sin management are doomed to fail. Only the power of God will do. In his book *Addiction and Grace*, Gerald May writes: "Ironically, freedom becomes most pure when our addictions have so confused and defeated us that we sense no choice left at all. Here, where we feel absolutely powerless, we have the most real power. Nothing is left in us to force us to choose one way or another. Our choice, then, is a true act of faith. We may put our faith in ourselves or in our attachments or in God."[9]

Put your faith in God and you will find true freedom. When you sin, do not turn away from the cross; run toward it. There you will meet a Savior who never sinned—not even once. Not that he was never tempted, though. The Bible says that Jesus was tempted in every way (Heb. 4:15), which presumably includes the temptations that David faced: lust, adultery, falsehood, murder, and every other deadly sin. With the help of the Spirit, Jesus found a way to escape all of these dangers and, as a result, his death on the cross was a perfect sacrifice.

Now the crucified, risen Lord Jesus offers us forgiveness and freedom. Many things can help us in our struggle with sin. Promises from Scripture, accountability partners, addiction-recovery groups, and the sacrament of the Lord's Supper all have their place. But the main thing that helps us is repentance with faith, in which we openly confess our sin and then hold on to the cross and believe in the mercy of Jesus. What brings spiritual change is the gospel, and everyone who believes the gospel receives the same blessing that King David once pronounced: "May the LORD answer you in the day of trouble! May the name of the God of Jacob protect you!" (Ps. 20:1).

5

"Cursed Be the Day I Was Born!"

Jeremiah's Disheartening Persecution

(Jeremiah 20:1–18)

It was at the upper Benjamin Gate of the temple in Jerusalem, and the prophet Jeremiah was in trouble. Real trouble. The night before, he had been put in prison. A man named Pashhur—the head of temple security and the chief of Israel's "prophecy police"—had taken exception to Jeremiah's message of judgment against Jerusalem. So he had seized the prophet, beat him, and then bound him.

The next day, Pashhur had a change of heart and removed Jeremiah's restraints. Once he had been released, the prophet pronounced words of divine judgment against his tormentor. According to the word of God that came to Jeremiah, Pashhur's friends would fall by the sword or else die in captivity (Jer. 20:4). His lies would be exposed and his crimes would be repaid with death (v. 6). Jeremiah even had the delicious satisfaction of giving Pashhur a nickname that was bound to stick. Pashhur means "Fruitful on Every Side," but Jeremiah called him "Magor-Missabib" (v. 3 NIV), which means "Terror on Every Side" (ESV).

Dark Night of the Soul

That is not the whole story, because it does not tell us what went through Jeremiah's mind during his long night in jail. For this, we need to read the soliloquy the prophet gives in Jeremiah 20:7–18, during his dark night of the soul. Jeremiah starts by lamenting everything that was going wrong in his life, which took a while:

> O Lord, you have deceived me,
>> and I was deceived;
> you are stronger than I,
>> and you have prevailed.
> I have become a laughingstock all the day;
>> everyone mocks me.
> For whenever I speak, I cry out,
>> I shout, "Violence and destruction!"
> For the word of the Lord has become for me
>> a reproach and derision all day long.
> If I say, "I will not mention him,
>> or speak any more in his name,"

there is in my heart as it were a burning fire
    shut up in my bones,
and I am weary with holding it in,
    and I cannot.
For I hear many whispering.
    Terror is on every side!
"Denounce him! Let us denounce him!"
    say all my close friends,
    watching for my fall.
"Perhaps he will be deceived;
    then we can overcome him
    and take our revenge on him." (vv. 7–10)

Then Jeremiah's mood unexpectedly shifts, as he puts his confidence in God and says:

But the LORD is with me as a dread warrior;
    therefore my persecutors will stumble;
    they will not overcome me. . . .
Sing to the LORD;
    praise the LORD!
For he has delivered the life of the needy
    from the hand of evildoers. (vv. 11, 13)

Then comes the surprise ending, in which Jeremiah utters some of the bitterest curses in the Bible before closing with a haunting question:

Cursed be the day
    on which I was born!
The day when my mother bore me,
    let it not be blessed! . . .

Why did I come out from the womb
    to see toil and sorrow,
    and spend my days in shame? (vv. 14, 18)

The writer Kathleen Norris first heard Jeremiah's words at St. John's Abbey in Minnesota. Norris lived with the monks of St. John's for a year and a half. During her stay, she discovered that an important part of monastic life is the continuous reading of entire books of the Bible, section by section, during morning and evening prayer. She writes:

> The most remarkable experience of all was plunging into the prophet Jeremiah at morning prayer in late September one year, and staying with him through mid-November. We began with chapter 1, and read straight through. . . . Listening to Jeremiah is one hell of a way to get your blood going in the morning; it puts caffeine to shame.[1]

Norris goes on to explain how Jeremiah's sufferings became the agonies of her own soul:

> Opening oneself to a prophet as anguished as Jeremiah is painful. On some mornings, I found it impossible. . . . The voice of Jeremiah is compelling, often on an overwhelmingly personal level. One morning, I was so worn out by the emotional roller coaster of chapter 20 that after prayers I walked to my apartment and went back to bed. This passionate soliloquy, which begins with a bitter outburst on the nature of the prophet's calling, moves quickly into denial. Jeremiah's anger at the way his enemies deride him rears up, and also fear and sorrow. His statement of confidence in God seems forced under the circumstances, and a brief doxology feels

more ironic than not, being followed by a bitter cry. The chapter concludes with an anguished question.[2]

Norris is right: Jeremiah 20 gives us plenty of reasons to dive back under the covers. It is the low point of the prophet's ministry, in which he does the same things that we are tempted to do when life seems to go against us: he blames God, rejects his calling in life, and curses the day he was born.

Take It to the Lord in Prayer

Jeremiah's words teach us at least three valuable lessons about what to do when trouble comes. The first may be the most important: *Take your troubles to the Lord in prayer.*

Jeremiah had many good reasons to be discouraged. For starters, he was in danger. Priests were gathering in the corners of the temple. Jeremiah could hear their nasty whispers and see their bony fingers pointed in his direction. Honestly, people were sick and tired of hearing his message of judgment (see v. 8). Even his so-called friends were waiting for him to take a false step so they could pounce on him. He had already been beaten and locked up. What would they do to him next?

The prophet was also discouraged because people were mocking him: "I have become a laughingstock all the day; everyone mocks me" (v. 7). The comedians in Jerusalem were getting some of their funniest material at Jeremiah's expense. Although their real issue was with the message, they started mocking the messenger: "There goes that crazy old prophet. Did you hear what he did yesterday? He took a brand new clay pot and smashed it outside the city walls. The guy needs a straightjacket. He keeps babbling about enemies coming to destroy our city."

Verbal abuse may not seem very serious compared to a vicious beating, but eventually ridicule starts to take its toll. One insult was especially vicious. They called Jeremiah Magor-Missabib, or "Terror On Every Side" (v. 10). In other words, they took his rebuke of Pashhur and used it against him.

Jeremiah was despised and rejected. His friends had betrayed him, including, it seemed, the closest of all friends. "O LORD," he lamented, "you have deceived me, and I was deceived; you are stronger than I, and you have prevailed" (v. 7). Apparently, Jeremiah was starting to doubt whether the Word of God was really true after all. God had compelled Jeremiah to prophesy, and so he had prophesied, but where was the judgment that God had promised? Really, it was God's fault that Jeremiah was suffering; the prophet was simply saying what God had told him to say. And the longer God waited before fulfilling his promise, the more Jeremiah wondered whether he had become a false prophet. Maybe the Lord had deceived him.

Has this ever happened to you when you were discouraged? Life is so hard that sometimes we start to wonder whether everything we have ever heard about God and about his gospel is really true. Maybe we have been fooled all along.

The only thing Jeremiah could think of to do with his doubts and troubles was to take them to the Lord in prayer. Chapter 20 is the prayer of a suffering believer. Imagine Jeremiah in solitary confinement, weakened with physical pain and exhausted by emotional turmoil. Yet the very first words out of his mouth are an invocation to almighty God. "O LORD," he cries. "O LORD!"

God invites us to take our troubles straight to him. This is what godly people have done throughout history. It is what Job did on the ash heap, when he was grieving the death of his family (Job 3). It is what David did in the cave, when he was hiding from King Saul (Psalm 57). It is what Jonah did in the belly of the whale, when he tried to run away from God (Jonah 2). It is even what Jesus did on the cross, when he was suffering for our sins. "My God, my God," he said (Matt. 27:46).

So whenever you are in trouble, take your troubles to a secret place where you can meet with God in prayer. Where else can you open your heart so freely? Who else will comfort you so tenderly? There is no need to hide your troubles. Take them to the Lord in prayer!

Call to Worship

As the prophet prayed, he took heart. The Holy Spirit was ministering to his soul. And so, suddenly and totally unexpectedly, he interrupted his complaint to hold a short worship service. Yes, he was alone and afraid, discouraged and disheartened. Nevertheless, in Jeremiah 20:11–13, he offered a psalm of praise to his God. This teaches us a second lesson: *Even when we are in trouble, God deserves our praise.*

Jeremiah's worship service may have been short, but it was complete. His psalm included a confession of faith, a prayer for deliverance, and a hymn of praise.

The prophet's confession of faith went like this:

> But the Lord is with me as a dread warrior;
> > therefore my persecutors will stumble;
> > they will not overcome me.
> They will be greatly shamed,
> > for they will not succeed. (v. 11)

Jeremiah really did not understand what was happening to him. Even God seemed to be against him. Yet he testified to what he knew to be true about the character of his Savior. In his comments on these verses, John Calvin writes: "Here the Prophet sets up God's aid against all the plottings formed against him. However, then, might perfidious friends on one hand try privately to entrap him, and open enemies might on the other hand publicly oppose him, he yet doubted not but that God would be a sufficient protection to him."[3]

Jeremiah believed that God was with him even when he seemed far away. He knew that the Lord was strong even though personally he felt powerless. He expected the wicked to be defeated even if they appeared to triumph. So the prophet boldly confessed that God would be his salvation.

What is the confession of your faith—not just the creed you recite in church, but the confidence you live by every day? In all your troubles, and in all the troubles of a fallen world, are you able to say that God is with you like a mighty warrior?

Jeremiah believed this, and because he believed it, he was ready to pray for help:

> O LORD of hosts, who tests the righteous,
>   who sees the heart and the mind,
> let me see your vengeance upon them,
>   for to you have I committed my cause. (v. 12)

When Jeremiah was in trouble, he did not take matters into his own hands. He did not try to solve his problems on his own. Instead, he committed his cause to the Lord. In his particular case, this meant praying that his cause would be vindicated and his enemies put to shame. Our cases may be different, but the principle is the same: if we believe that God is with us and that he has the power to help us, then we should ask him for all the help that only he can give.

Jeremiah believed in God's deliverance so strongly that he closed his time of worship with a hymn of praise. Suddenly, the prophet burst into song:

> Sing to the LORD;
>> praise the LORD!
> For he has delivered the life of the needy
>> from the hand of evildoers. (v. 13)

We can imagine Jeremiah bent over in his stocks as he sings. He may not have had the breath to sing a long anthem, but at least he could manage one short song of praise. He came through his doubts to a place of such strong confidence in the Lord that he praised God during his dark night of the soul. It is also possible that Jeremiah added this stanza to his song *after* he was released from prison. Either way, notice that the psalm refers to the needy person in the singular. Literally, the Lord rescues the life "of the needy one" (v. 13), meaning the prophet himself.

Like Jeremiah, the German theologian Dietrich Bonhoeffer was imprisoned for the sake of God's Word. Bonhoeffer endured his dark night of the soul in a Nazi concentration camp. Yet even there, he did not stop praising God. Instead, he prayed:

> In me there is darkness,
>> but with Thee there is light.
> I am lonely, but Thou leavest me not.

I am restless, but with Thee there is peace.
In me there is bitterness, but with Thee there is patience;
Thy ways are past understanding,
> but Thou knowest the way for me.[4]

It is always good to praise the Lord, but especially so when we are in trouble. The best thing to do when we are discouraged and disheartened is to worship. Keep confessing, keep praying, keep singing. Even when you have a complaint to make, confess your faith in God, pray for deliverance, and praise his name.

The Final Question

It is tempting to stop right here, with Jeremiah's psalm of praise, but that is not how the story ends. The Bible must be taken as it comes, and this time it ends on a downer. As the last note of his song is fading away, the prophet tells us that he wants to die:

Cursed be the day
> on which I was born!
The day when my mother bore me,
> let it not be blessed!
Cursed be the man who brought the news to my father,
"A son is born to you,"
> making him very glad.
Let that man be like the cities
> that the LORD overthrew without pity;
let him hear a cry in the morning
> and an alarm at noon,
because he did not kill me in the womb;
> so my mother would have been my grave,
> and her womb forever great. (Jer. 20:14–17)

Instead of celebrating his birthday, Jeremiah cursed it. He wanted to reach back into history and curse everything and everyone who had anything to do with his birth. In fact, he wished the man who had brought his father the "good news" had strangled him instead.

Jeremiah's mood swung from praising to cursing with dizzying speed. One verse is a psalm of high praise; the next is a lament of utter despair. This has led some scholars to conclude that verse 14 "can hardly belong after verse 13."[5] They view chapter 20 as a hodgepodge of the prophet's sayings. Even Calvin is mystified; to him, it seems "unworthy of the holy man to pass suddenly from thanksgiving to God into imprecations, as though he had forgotten himself."[6]

Perhaps Jeremiah had forgotten himself, but these verses *do* belong together. They may not belong together by logic, but who says the life of the soul is always logical? Jeremiah's curses follow his praises because that is the way it was during his dark night of the soul.

It is important for us to recognize the confusing, sometimes schizophrenic nature of the Christian life. We are at one and the same time saints and sinners. Although our sins are forgiven, we continue to sin. Furthermore, our lives contain a mixture of pains and pleasures. So one minute we praise and the next minute we curse; one day we rejoice in God's plan for us and the very next day we resist his purposes.

Jeremiah's curses form one of the bitterest laments in the Bible. Derek Kidner observes that the prophet's words are intended "to bowl us over. Together with other tortured cries from him and his fellow sufferers, these raw wounds in Scripture remain lest we forget the sharpness of the age-long struggle, or the frailty of the finest overcomers."[7]

Notice that Jeremiah stopped just short of cursing God, or his parents, which were both capital offenses in Israel (Lev. 20:9; 24:15–16). He was not exactly thinking about ending it all, but he did wish that it had never started. So he asked this question:

> Why did I come out from the womb
>> to see toil and sorrow,
>> and spend my days in shame? (v. 18)

Jeremiah had known the suffering of persecution, the sorrow of watching his people reject God's Word, and the shame of public humiliation. All of these troubles placed a huge question mark over his existence. Although the prophet was strong in his faith, there were times when he had more questions than answers. Here he queried just about everything: his creation, his salvation, and his vocation.[8]

If we think about Jeremiah's questions in their total biblical context, they teach us one final lesson: *Although our troubles can place a giant question mark over our existence, they never have the last word.*

Chapter 20 ends with a question that Jeremiah himself was in no shape to answer, but Scripture does provide an answer. Why *did* Jeremiah come out of the womb to see trouble and sorrow?

God gave Jeremiah the answer back at the very beginning, when he first called him into ministry. The prophet needed to be reminded of the first thing that God ever said to him:

Before I formed you in the womb I knew you,
and before you were born I consecrated you;
I appointed you a prophet to the nations. (1:5)

Jeremiah traced his troubles back to his mother's womb. But he did not go back far enough! God traced his promises back even further, before the womb. He had a purpose for Jeremiah's life from before the beginning of time. The prophet needed to be reminded that the Lord had set him apart for salvation and for ministry from all eternity.

Maybe we need the same reminder. Every day we suffer. Sometimes we are ridiculed by friends or family members, or enemies wait to trip us up. We are weighed down by the ungodliness we see around us in society and the church. There are times when we wonder why we ever came out of the womb.

This is why: God set us apart for salvation and for ministry. Before the beginning of time, he planned to save us in Jesus Christ. The Bible says that "he [God] chose us in him [Jesus] before the foundation of the world" (Eph. 1:4). God also set us apart to do his work in the world. "We are his workmanship," the Bible says, "created in Christ Jesus for good works, which God prepared beforehand, that we should walk in them" (Eph. 2:10). Even when trouble places a giant question mark over our existence, God's plan for us and grace for us in Jesus Christ always have the last word.

This does not mean that we always get a simple, satisfying answer to all of our questions about suffering. In a 2014 testimony about his experience with a debilitating disease, Wheaton College Provost Stan Jones provided a helpful perspective on all the questions about our suffering that we find difficult or even impossible to answer. He said:

Long ago, I read a book about suffering, and the author made a point that I have had to return to time and time again. He said most of our why questions about suffering are ultimately unanswerable. God does not seem to be in the business of answering the why questions, and most of our philosophical responses to the question of suffering amount to various forms of taking God off the hook for the problem of suffering. But this author pointed out that God doesn't seem to be interested in getting off the hook. In fact, the answer of God in Jesus Christ to the problem of suffering is not to get off the hook at all, but rather to impale himself on the hook of human suffering with us in the very midst of our suffering.[9]

When trouble comes and places a giant question mark over our existence, we should remember Jesus and the empathy of the cross.

"A Sword Will Pierce Your Own Soul Too"

Mary's Troubled Soul
(Luke 1:26–38; 2:22–35)

It was during the betrothal—sometime after the engagement and not too long before the wedding—and Mary was in trouble. Real trouble. She was at home in the city of Nazareth, minding her own business, when suddenly an angel appeared to her and said, "Greetings, O favored one, the Lord is with you!" (Luke 1:28). This may not sound like trouble, but only to people who have never seen a real, live angel before. Mary did see an angel, and she "was greatly troubled at the saying, and tried to discern what sort of greeting this might be" (v. 29). The poor girl must have seemed as if she was scared half to death, because the angel took one look at her and sensed the need to offer immediate reassurance: "Do not be afraid, Mary, for you have found favor with God" (v. 30).

Mary's Baby

The angel's words were full of blessing. He called Mary by name and gave her his salutations. He said that God was with her and had grace for her. He declared that she was in favor with God. But Mary was still right to be troubled, because she was about to receive God's call, and with it the unimaginable sufferings that would trouble her every day from Christmas to Easter. Being divinely favored does not mean that God will spare you from every trouble. Often the trouble is just beginning.

Mary's troubles began with what the angel told her was about to happen: "And behold, you will conceive in your womb and bear a son, and you shall call his name Jesus. He will be great and will be called the Son of the Most High. And the Lord God will give to him the throne of his father David, and he will reign over the house of Jacob forever, and of his kingdom there will be no end" (Luke 1:31–33).

The angel packed a lot of promises into one short speech, but the main thing that Mary heard was the part about having a baby. "You're kidding, right?" she might have said. Mary hadn't even finished planning her wedding yet, and she had never . . . you know . . . been with a man before. She knew enough about the facts of life to ask the obvious question: "How will this be, since I am a virgin?" (v. 34).

The angel had a good answer—at least, for anyone who believes in the Word of God, the power of the Holy Spirit, and the mystery of the incarnation. But however good it was, it wasn't an easy answer. The angel told Mary: "The Holy Spirit will come upon you, and the power of the Most High will over-shadow you; therefore the child to be born will be called holy—the Son of God. . . . For nothing will be impossible with God" (vv. 35, 37).

The angel thus explained how God could do this, but he didn't explain how Mary could deal with it. Talk about a prob-lem pregnancy! Anyone who thinks getting pregnant was any-thing but a heap of trouble for a nice girl like Mary has never lived in a small town like Nazareth. People there could do a little arithmetic, starting at nine months and counting back-ward. Before long, they would know that Mary was farther along than she was supposed to be, and people do have a way of talking.

Then there was all the trouble that Mary had with the child-birth. Like many couples in those days, Joseph and Mary were tossed around by the powerful machine of Roman geopolitics. Caesar declared a census, and off they went to pay their taxes, trudging to Bethlehem, or maybe riding on a donkey. When they arrived, Mary discovered that Joseph had failed to secure a reservation. No Expedia, apparently; no booking.com. So they made do with what they had and bedded down in a stable. There, Mary's water broke and she gave birth to her firstborn son. The delivery must have been agony. It always is—agony before ecstasy. The new mother knew that God had kept his promise. Shepherds came to celebrate the good news with great joy. But none of this was easy.

A few weeks later, the happy couple made their way to Jerusalem to dedicate their baby at the temple. They didn't have much to offer—just a pair of baby pigeons, which is what poor people brought in those days. Simeon the priest took the baby Jesus into his arms and blessed him. But then he turned to Mary and said: "This child is destined to cause the falling and rising of many in Israel, and to be a sign that will be spoken against, so that the thoughts of many hearts will be revealed. And a sword will pierce through your own soul too" (Luke 2:34–35 NIV).

Mary hardly knew what Simeon was saying. But she understood enough to know that his words were casting a long, dark shadow over her maternity. Her precious, beloved son would divide the heart of the nation. Some people would love him, but others would hate him. All of this would drive a dagger straight through Mary's heart—the heart of a mother who loved her son as only a mother could.

Soon there was more trouble. When King Herod learned that a new king had been born to the Jews, he flew into a jealous rage and took out a contract on Mary's newborn son. The family needed to get as far away as possible, so they started off on another long trip. This time they went all the way to Egypt. Mary and Joseph were poor. They were the victims of persecution. They were homeless refugees. They were undocumented immigrants. Whatever categories we might use to describe them, they suffered all the kinds of trouble that people face when they are on the margin between life and death.

In December 2014, the television program *60 Minutes* aired a segment on the plight of refugees fleeing war-torn Syria to find sanctuary in Jordan. Army trucks were parked at the border to carry the refugees to a camp where they would find food and water. There was enough room on the trucks for everyone, but the mothers would not wait: they put all their children on the first truck they saw, even if it meant staying behind. If there was any risk, they would run it themselves and send their children ahead to safety.

Mary must have felt the same way. Whatever danger she faced—in Nazareth, in Bethlehem, in Jerusalem, and in Egypt— her one thought was to protect her son. She was called to raise him up for the work of the kingdom, whatever trouble it took.

Mary's Man-Child

The Christmas story was not the end of Mary's troubles, but only the beginning. Jesus was a good boy. In fact, the Bible makes a point of saying that he obeyed his parents (Luke 2:51). But it can't have been easy, either for Jesus or for his mother. As Jesus was growing up, his unique identity as the Son of God and his unique calling as the Savior of the world put a constant strain on his family ties.

Recall what happened when Jesus was twelve and his family went up to Jerusalem for Passover. This annual pilgrimage was a family tradition that must have been a great experience for a boy like Jesus. The streets of the city were crammed with two hundred thousand worshipers and one hundred thousand sacrificial lambs. By the time he was twelve, Jesus would have had the run of the city, with all its sights and sounds.

In another year, he would be thirteen, the age at which he would become a full member of the synagogue—a "son of the law," or *bar mitzvah*. According to custom, a boy of twelve would go up to Jerusalem with his father and become a man by learning the sacred rituals of Passover.

This was the context for a famous mix-up: "When the feast was ended, as they were returning, the boy Jesus stayed behind in Jerusalem. His parents did not know it, but supposing him to be in the group they went a day's journey, but then they began to search for him among their relatives and acquaintances, and when they did not find him, they returned to Jerusalem, searching for him" (Luke 2:43–45).

It is not hard to guess how this happened. For reasons of safety and fellowship, the pilgrims did not travel as individual families, but in large caravans. Typically, the women went on ahead with the younger children, and the men came along afterward. At age twelve, Jesus would have been a "'tweener." Mary perhaps thought he was traveling with the men for the first time, while Joseph may well have assumed that he was still with his mother.

By the time they stopped for the night, the Messiah was missing. Mary must have been in an absolute panic. Almost nothing is more frightening for a mother than to lose a child. It has happened to our family in Center City Philadelphia and then again in West Virginia. Both times, only a few minutes passed till we found the child. But no one in our family will ever forget the eternity of fear that gripped us in a single moment.

"Where's Jesus?" "Has anyone seen Jesus?" "When was the last time you saw him?" It took an entire day to travel back to Jerusalem. Mary must have made the journey with a lump in her throat and an ache in her mother's heart.

Mary and Joseph needed three days to find Jesus—three days! They finally found him at the temple, talking theology with the leading Bible scholars in Israel. Mary was relieved, of course, but we can tell from what she said that she felt exactly the way any mother feels when a child goes missing. She was angry—angry enough to scold Jesus right on the spot: "Son, why have you treated us so? Behold, your father and I have been searching for you in great distress" (Luke 2:48).

Spoken like a true mother. Even the phrasing sounds familiar—everything from "your father and I" to "Why have you treated us so?" By appealing to her emotions, Mary made it perfectly clear that what Jesus had done had troubled her soul.

In point of fact, Jesus was right where he should have been. But what the boy said was another dagger through Mary's heart: "Why were you looking for me? Did you not know that I must be in my Father's house?" (v. 49).

Things would only get worse from there. Jesus left the family business to become a traveling preacher. Anyone who thinks that this was easy has never had a child quit a steady job in order to freelance. One of the first things Jesus did in his new career was to alienate his neighbors, who promptly drove him out of town (Luke 4:28–30). This, too, must have been something for people to talk about when they gathered at the well in Nazareth and shared the town gossip.

Then there was the time when Mary tried to help Jesus get started in ministry. They were at a wedding in Cana, and the host had run out of wine. Mary wanted her son to do something about it. Mothers are like that: they always have "suggestions" for what their children should do. But Jesus said to her: "Dear woman, why do you involve me? My time has not yet come" (John 2:4 NIV).

Or what about the time when Mary and the rest of her boys heard that Jesus was teaching in a nearby town? Frankly, they were worried about him. Some people thought he was the Messiah, but other people thought he was out of his mind, and some people probably wanted to kill him. As usual, a large crowd had gathered to hear Jesus preach. Mary wanted to speak with Jesus—maybe out of concern for his well-being—but she couldn't get anywhere close. When someone tugged on his sleeve to let him know that his mother was waiting to see him, Jesus put another dagger through Mary's heart by saying, "Who is my mother, and who are my brothers?" (Matt. 12:48). Then he pointed to his disciples and said, "Here are my mother and my brothers!" (v. 49).

But all of these blades were only table knives compared to the broadsword that pierced Mary's heart at Calvary, where her beloved, innocent son was executed by crucifixion! Mary took her place next to the cross (John 19:25). Think of it: she watched her son get tortured to death. Up until that moment, she may well have expected that her amazing son, with all of his miraculous powers, would find some way to escape the cross. But she was there when they stripped him naked and gambled for his robe. She was there when they nailed him to the tree and lifted him up to die. She was there to see the blood, to hear the mockers, and to feel the cold shadow of the wrath of God. And when a sword pierced his side, she was close enough to feel its sharp edge somewhere deep in her soul.

What Mary Did

Has any mother ever suffered more deeply than Mary, the mother of Jesus? Her life story hardly fits the expected pattern for someone who is "favored" by God. A poem by Thomas Warton the Elder captures something of Mary's excruciating suffering in losing her son at the cross:

Beneath, lo! Mary weeping stands,
In tears more pitifully fair,
And beats the breast, where Christ had hung,
And tears her long disheveled hair—
"Where can I lay my mournful head?
My son, my king, my God is dead!"[1]

So how did Mary bear all of these sorrows? And what can we learn from her example about what to do when trouble comes?

The best way to answer these questions is to go back to what Mary said when God called her to give birth to his only Son. At first, she was troubled by the angel's greeting. She also had some good, honest questions about how a virgin could possibly conceive and bear a child. But when the angel told her that the Holy Spirit would overshadow her, and when she was reminded that nothing is impossible with God, she totally surrendered. Her simple declaration of obedience is a model for our submission to the will of God: "Behold, I am the servant of the Lord; let it be to me according to your word" (Luke 1:38).

There were a lot of other things that Mary could have done when trouble came. She could have refused to obey. She could have told God that she was available for easy jobs, but not for hard jobs. Out of weakness or fear, she could have said: "Here am I, Lord. Send somebody else!"

Another thing that Mary could have done was to negotiate. She could have pressed for more details about exactly what God was asking her to do. Then she could have asked for certain reassurances about what God would do for her. "I'll think about it, Lord," she might have said, "but is there any chance that you would be willing to speak with my fiancé first?" Or she might have told God that she would do it on one condition, namely, that he wouldn't give more than she could bear.

Later, when all the troubles started to come, Mary could have questioned the goodness of God. When Herod was killing babies and her little family was exiled to Egypt, she could have criticized God for failing to protect his people. That long and desperate journey was only the beginning. By the time Jesus reached the cross, Mary could have produced a long list of grievances against the Almighty, ending with the soul-piercing crucifixion of her beloved son. At any point along the way, she could have told God that she just wasn't going to do it anymore—his plan was too much trouble.

Have you ever felt that way—like you wanted out? Has life let you down so badly and so frequently that you just didn't want to follow God any longer?

If Mary was tempted that way, she never gave in. Instead, she remained absolutely devoted to God. Step by painful step, she followed the path of suffering that had been marked out for her. How did she do it? What was her secret? When trouble came, as trouble does, how did she endure?

The answer lies partly in the decision that Mary made before her trouble came. As soon as she understood what God wanted her to do, she simply said, "Behold, I am the servant of the Lord; let it be to me according to your word" (Luke 1:38). As a woman of faith, Mary surrendered her body and her soul to the living God. She did not insist on knowing all the details or negotiate for better terms. She did not place any conditions on her service to God—things she wouldn't do or places she wouldn't go. His word was her command. So she simply said, "Do as you will, Lord."

Doing what God said came naturally to Mary because her life had been deeply shaped by meditating on the Word of God. We know this because her famous song—"the Magnificat"—is comprised of verse after verse from the Psalms (see Luke 1:46–55). Mary not only knew the Psalms, but she had also taken to heart their deep, inner logic of firm confidence in the character and promises of God.

So when the time came for Mary to give her life to God, she gave her whole life to him, holding nothing in reserve. When she said yes to the virgin birth, she also meant yes to the stable in Bethlehem, yes to the exile in Egypt, yes to losing Jesus in Jerusalem, yes to people hating her son and thinking he was crazy, even yes to the crucifixion, the burial, and the grave. Whenever Mary was doubtful or discouraged, disheartened or disillusioned, she could look back to the commitment she had made with full confidence in the purposes of God: "Behold, I am the servant of the Lord; let it be to me according to your word."

Following Mary's Example

What commitment have you made? Are you a servant of the Lord, as Mary was? Have you offered your body and your soul to the kingdom purposes of Jesus Christ, whatever trouble may come?

Don't give up and don't give in. Keep offering your life for the plans and purposes of God. He will be as faithful to you as he was to Mary.

In her drama *The Man Born to Be King*, Dorothy L. Sayers imagined a conversation between Mary and one of the magi who came to worship Jesus at his cradle. The wise man was weighed down by suffering, and wondered where God was in life's troubles. He said:

I speak for a sorrowful people—for the ignorant and the poor. We rise up to labour and lie down to sleep, and night is only a pause between one burden and another. Fear is our daily companion—the fear of want, the fear of war, the fear of cruel death, and of still more cruel life. But all this we could bear if we knew that we did not suffer in vain; that God was beside us in the struggle, sharing the miseries of His own world. For the riddle that torments the world is this: Shall Sorrow and Love be reconciled at last, when the promised Kingdom comes?

The reply that Sayers puts in Mary's mouth rings true to her experience of God's grace, as recorded in the Gospels:

These are very difficult questions—but with me, you see, it is like this. When the Angel's message came to me, the Lord put a song into my heart. I suddenly saw that wealth and cleverness were nothing to God—no one is too unimportant to be His friend. That was the thought that came to me, because of the thing that happened to *me*. I am quite humbly born, yet the Power of God came upon me; very foolish and unlearned, yet the Word of God was spoken to me; and I was in deep distress, when my Baby was born and filled my life with love. So I know very well that Wisdom and Power and

Sorrow *can* live together with Love; and for me, the Child in my arms is the answer to all the riddles.[2]

In every trouble she faced, God was with Mary to help her. When she was troubled by the angel's first greeting, God spoke words of comfort: "Do not be afraid. . . . Nothing will be impossible with God." When Herod sent his soldiers to do their deadly work, God protected Mary's baby. He was with the mother and child on their journey to Egypt, and he brought them safely back to Nazareth. When Mary thought that Jesus was lost, God kept him safe in the temple. When Jesus was dying on the cross, he made sure that Mary would be well cared for by tenderly entrusting her to the apostle John, his beloved disciple (John 19:26–27).

Three days later, Jesus came back from the dead, and Mary's troubles were over. Hallelujah!

The last glimpse we catch of her comes after Jesus ascended to heaven and his disciples gathered for prayer in the upper room. Mary was there with them (Acts 1:13–14), worshiping the God that she had served her entire life—the God who was with her through every trouble.

The Holy Spirit invites us to make Mary's commitment our own, and to say: "I am your servant, Lord. Do with me whatever you will. Let it be to me according to your word." People who make this commitment usually face all kinds of trouble. But when trouble comes—danger, exile, abandonment, even death—we will be kept safe in the love of God. And we will be able to offer the same exultant praise that Mary gave: "He who is mighty has done great things for me" (Luke 1:49).

"Now Is My Soul Troubled"

The Savior's Suffering unto Death

(John 12:20–33)

It was four or five days before the Last Supper—on the same day as our Savior's Triumphal Entry into Jerusalem—and Jesus (yes, Jesus) was in trouble. Real trouble. We know this not simply from what transpired over the course of that momentous week, but also because Jesus said it himself—out loud—to Andrew and Philip, and maybe to some of the other disciples: "Now is my soul troubled" (John 12:27a).

Why "Now"?

Of all the times when Jesus could have said that he was in trouble, why did he say it at precisely this moment?

John begins this chapter by saying that it was "six days before the Passover." Jesus was staying in Bethany, not far from
Jerusalem, with his friends Mary and Martha and their brother,
Lazarus. The next day, he rode a donkey into the Holy City,
where crowds welcomed him as their Messiah—especially people who had heard that he had raised Lazarus from the dead (see
John 12:17–18). "Hosanna!" they shouted. "Blessed is he who
comes in the name of the Lord!" (v. 13).

The Pharisees were offended by this and said, "Look, the
world has gone after him" (v. 19). It was true: everyone wanted
to follow Jesus, including some Gentiles who wanted to meet the
Messiah in person. They must have been a little bashful, though,
because rather than speaking to Jesus directly, they approached
one of his disciples instead. They spoke with Philip, who was
from Galilee and probably knew how to speak Greek, as they
did. They said to him, "Sir, we wish to see Jesus" (v. 21).

Those were thrilling days, when people wanted to see, follow, and worship Jesus. Nevertheless, the Savior knew that he
was in trouble. "My soul is troubled," he said. The question is:
Why did he say this now?

Jesus could have said this at many points in his life, and it
would have made perfect sense. He was in trouble even before
he was born, as we saw in the previous chapter, where we looked
at his mother, Mary, and all her troubles. Jesus was born to a
virgin, which meant that there would always be rumors about
his parentage—accusations that he was illegitimate. When the
time came for him to be born, there was no room for him at the
inn, only a manger in a stable.

The child was in danger almost immediately after he was

born. King Herod took out a contract on him when he was a baby, of all things, so Jesus had to be taken all the way to Egypt for safety. Eventually his family returned to Israel and lived a quiet life in the town of Nazareth. By all accounts, Jesus had a happy childhood. But there was trouble as soon as he began his public ministry.

Jesus was in trouble out in the wilderness, where he fasted forty days and forty nights. There he came under the direct attack of Satan, who tempted him to use his power for his personal advantage, to seek his kingdom without suffering (Matt. 4:1–11).

After resisting these deadly temptations, Jesus went back to Nazareth and started preaching the gospel according to Isaiah—the good news of freedom for the poor (Luke 4:18ff.). His neighbors loved what he had to say—until he started telling them that God had grace for Gentiles, too. As soon as they heard this, they tried to execute him for blasphemy (vv. 28–30).

The more miracles Jesus performed, the more popular he became and the more certain religious leaders tried to find fault with him. Some called him a heretic, others a lunatic. They not only criticized him, but they also started to plot against him, looking for some way to put him to death.

Neither were these the only troubles that Jesus faced. Consider the burden he carried for people who were lost and helpless, like sheep without a shepherd (Matt. 9:36). Consider the lament he offered for Jerusalem—the city that he longed to bring under his loving protection (Matt. 23:37–39). Consider the intense emotions that he felt at the tomb of Lazarus, where he wept for the loss that his friends had suffered and wailed against the ravages that death brings to fallen humanity (John 11:35, 38). Consider the tears he shed during his Triumphal Entry into Jerusalem; while the crowds were cheering, Jesus wept openly over the rejection of his people and the destruction that would come to the Holy City as a result (Luke 19:41–44).

By the time Jesus came to the last week of his life, he had suffered many troubles. He was homeless, an outcast. He was "a man of sorrows, and acquainted with grief" (Isa. 53:3). He seemed to be in trouble almost all the time. Yet this was the moment in the Gospels when he opened a window into his heart and said, "Now is my soul troubled."

The reason is very simple. None of the trials that Jesus had faced thus far could possibly measure up to the terror of the cross. Right before saying that his soul was troubled, Jesus had said this: "Truly, truly, I say to you, unless a grain of wheat falls into the earth and dies, it remains alone; but if it dies, it bears much fruit. Whoever loves his life loses it, and whoever hates his life in this world will keep it for eternal life" (John 12:24–25). Jesus was thinking about his death, burial, and resurrection. *He* was the grain of wheat that would fall into the ground and die, before rising again with the fruit of everlasting life.

Jesus could see what lay ahead of him. He knew that he was coming close to the greatest trouble that anyone would ever suffer. To be sure, he wasn't thinking about himself alone; he was also thinking about his disciples and the troubles that they were about to go through. But he was thinking about his own situation enough to admit that his soul was deeply troubled. On his darkest day, the psalmist had said, "My soul is full of troubles, and my life draws near to Sheol" (Ps. 88:3; cf. 6:3;

22:11). When Jesus felt the same way, he simply said, "Now is my soul troubled."

A Couple of Questions

As soon as Jesus said this—giving voice to his troubled soul—he asked himself the question that we have been asking ourselves throughout this book. He asked it right out loud, so his disciples could overhear it. He said, "And what shall I say?" (John 12:27b). In other words, "What shall I do when this trouble comes?"

Jesus followed his first question with a second, closely related question. He wondered if he should pray, "Father, save me from this hour" (v. 27c). For Jesus, this was a rhetorical question, but for most people it wouldn't be a question at all; it would be more of a demand: "Father, save me from this hour!"

Most people try to avoid trouble at any cost, and when it comes, we try to get out of it as soon as we can. This explains why some people say that they don't have any troubles or pretend that their troubles are over before they really are. Nobody likes to be in trouble. So when trouble comes, one of our first instincts is to ask God to get us out of trouble. There is nothing wrong with this, of course, as long as we recognize that God may have a more important purpose than simply getting us out of trouble.

When Jesus saw that trouble was coming, naturally he wondered if there was some way out. And he didn't stop thinking about this, either. The thought came back to him more than once during the last week of his first earthly life. "Maybe there's another way," he thought to himself. "Maybe there is some way out of the cross and around the grave."

115

For instance, these thoughts came back to Jesus the night when he was betrayed. As he was sharing dinner with his disciples that night—the Last Supper—he was "troubled in his spirit" (John 13:21). Similarly, Mark tells us that when Jesus went out to pray that night, he was "greatly distressed and troubled" (Mark 14:33). In fact, Jesus admitted this to some of his disciples. "My soul is very sorrowful," he said, "even to death" (v. 34). As he agonized in prayer, sweating blood and crying out to heaven, Jesus wondered if there was any other way to save his people. "If you are willing," he prayed to his Father, "remove this cup from me" (Luke 22:42).

Understand that Jesus was in trouble—real trouble. This means that Jesus understands—really understands—what it is like to be in trouble. I refer not to the kind of trouble we get into when we do the wrong thing, but to the kind that comes even when we do the right thing and are desperate to find some way out.

Have you ever been in that kind of trouble? Have you ever felt as if your whole world was falling apart? Have you ever felt as if something terrible was about to happen and you were powerless to prevent it? Have you ever felt as if there was no way out and no place to turn?

Jesus felt the same way, more than once. He sometimes had a troubled soul. And if we rightly understand the implications of the incarnation—that Jesus is fully human as well as fully divine—then it wasn't any easier for him to be in trouble than it is for us. In fact, the Bible says that "in the days of his flesh, Jesus offered up prayers and supplications, with loud cries and tears" (Heb. 5:7). It also describes our Savior as someone "who in every respect has been tempted as we are" (Heb. 4:15)—a description that surely includes the natural temptation to run away from trouble.

This means that when we go to Jesus with our troubles, we are not going to someone who *doesn't* understand, but to someone who *does*. Jesus can do a lot more than sympathize with us; he can empathize. And because he can empathize, he can show us—better than anyone else—what to do when trouble comes. "Because he himself has suffered when tempted," the Bible says, "he is able to help those who are being tempted" (Heb. 2:18).

In his song "Hard to Get," Rich Mullins has a few questions that he would like to have answered, as most of us do. The singer finds God "just plain hard to get" and somewhat out of touch with a world in pain. So he asks God: "Did You ever know loneliness / Did You ever know need / Do You remember just how long night can get?"

The answer is that Jesus knows these and many other troubles. Deep down, Mullins knows this, and so he sings:

> And I know you bore our sorrows
> And I know you feel our pain
> And I know it would not hurt any less
> Even if it could be explained
> And I know that I am only lashing out
> At the One who loves me most.[1]

The Savior who loves us the most is the One who understands us the best, and this is partly because he was in trouble, too. Here is how David Powlison explains the empathy that Jesus has for us:

He was not above it all. He entered our grievous plight. A man of sorrows, intimately acquainted with grief, enters into the hard places and comes under the afflictions. Jesus himself has never gotten over his experience of evil. He never got over it. It gives shape to his love, his courage, and his purposefulness. Jesus' friends recognized him when he invited them to "See my hands and my feet" (Luke 24:39–41). They saw the marks of the nails. But Jesus was not deformed by what he suffered. . . . He did not explode with darkness when he was trapped by darkness. Jesus was not defined by pain, but he does not forget what it is like. He did not return evil for evil, but he is merciful to those who do. He gets us.[2]

The Savior's Answer

So what did Jesus do when he was in trouble? How did he answer his rhetorical question?

Rather than trying to get out of trouble, Jesus embraced the calling of the cross. He said: "Now is my soul troubled. And what shall I say? 'Father, save me from this hour'? But for this purpose I have come to this hour" (John 12:27).

Jesus answered his own rhetorical question with a giant no! He refused to ask to be rescued from the dark hour of a bloody cross. Instead, he declared his immovable resolve to do whatever salvation required. This was the reason the Savior had come into the world: to save his people from their sins. So rather than turning away, as he was tempted to do, he went forward to Calvary and the crucifixion.

This meant that whatever trouble Jesus had faced up to this point was only the beginning. Sometimes our lives are like that, too. We do what God calls us to do, and then, rather than having less trouble in life, we have more. The more we serve, the more we have to sacrifice.

This is how it was for Jesus. Trouble came, and then trouble came again. Just a few short days after Jesus said that his soul was troubled, he was betrayed with a midnight kiss. He was unjustly arrested and falsely accused. Over the course of one long, agonizing night, he was dragged from one trial to the next. In those show trials—both religious and political—he was convicted of crimes he did not commit. Then he was beaten savagely before suffering death by torture.

Along the way, Jesus was ridiculed for being exactly who he was. The truest of all prophets was mocked for being a prophet. Before they handed him over to the Romans, some of his Jewish tormentors slapped him in the face and then said: "Prophesy to us, you Christ! Who is it that struck you?" (Matt. 26:68).

People mocked his kingship, too. When Roman soldiers led Jesus to his death, they scoffed at his royal claims with a scarlet robe, a thorny crown, and a scepter of straw. In mock homage, they knelt before him and said, "Hail, King of the Jews!" (Matt. 27:28–29).

Later that day, while he was offering his life as an atonement for sin, people scorned the efficacy of his priestly ministry. "He saved others," they said; "let him save himself, if he is the Christ of God, his Chosen One!" (Luke 23:35). At the very moment they said this, Jesus was performing the priestly ministry of prayer and sacrifice. The Great High Priest was interceding for the forgiveness of his enemies (Luke 23:34) and offering his body and his blood as a sacrifice for their sins. Nevertheless, they mocked him.

Has anyone ever had more trouble than Jesus Christ, who suffered all the way to death? What makes these tribulations especially remarkable is that, as the perfect Son of God, he never deserved to suffer at all, and he never would have suffered unless he had chosen by his own free will to enter this fallen world.

Consider how Jesus suffered many of the ugliest evils that we still see in the world today: unlawful incarceration; the slurs of anti-Semitism; racially motivated violence; hatred as an enemy without just cause; mockery; death by torture; and, in that brutal death, the shame of people seeing him naked.

I ask again: has anyone ever experienced more trouble than Jesus? And does anyone's suffering have more relevance for a world in pain—everywhere from the slums of India and Mexico City to the war-torn Middle East, from poverty-stricken Africa to inner-city America? Any Christian who is concerned about injustice, who calls for racial reconciliation, who cares for the survivors of sexual abuse, or who cries out because of the burnings and beheadings of the persecuted church knows a Savior who has a heart for the suffering—a heart that bled with redemption on the cross. Whatever answers Jesus has for the problems of the world came through the greatest suffering anyone has ever known.

The Highest Motivation

So why did Jesus go through with it? What empowered him to persevere? What motivated him to carry on with his calling, even when it meant nothing but trouble?

John shows us that Jesus was motivated by the highest of all ambitions: the glory of God. Notice how Jesus prayed. When his soul was troubled, he thought about saying, "Father, save me from this hour" (John 12:27c), but decided against it. Instead, he said, "Father, glorify your name" (v. 28).

When Jesus prayed this way, he was surrendering to his Father's plans and purposes. He was looking up to heaven and saying, "Thy will be done," which was really a way of asking for trouble, because the Father's wise purpose for him was suffering and death. Jesus knew this, because just a few verses later he prophesied that he would be "lifted up" to die (vv. 32–33). Jesus was willing to endure execution by crucifixion because his life was for the greater glory of God. He did not pursue his own pleasure; his primary purpose was to give glory to his Father.

This is exactly what the Savior did: he glorified God. And so, in a terrible and wonderful way, his prayers were answered. Through the sufferings and death of his one and only Son, God the Father glorified his name, just as he had promised (see v. 28). Jesus did not get out of trouble, but went through it, and everything he went through brought glory to God. Even the cross was for the glory of God. "There is no tribunal so magnificent," wrote John Calvin, "no throne so stately, no show of triumph so distinguished, no chariot so elevated, as is the gibbet on which Christ has subdued death and the devil."[3] As a result of what Jesus suffered on that cross, and then gained through the empty grave, our hearts are changed. Our guilt is forgiven. Our sins are washed away. Our lives have new purpose in the kingdom of God. Our place in heaven is secure forever.

All of this brings glory to God—the glory we give in the name of Jesus Christ. Here is how Kenya's "Masai Creed" expresses glory to God for the death and resurrection of Jesus Christ. It declares that after the Savior had been "tortured and nailed hands and feet to a cross, and died, he laid buried in the grave, but the hyenas did not touch him, and on the third day, he rose from the grave. He ascended unto the skies. He is the Lord!"[4]

Even when Christians use a creed that leaves out the hyenas, we praise God for the same salvation. The reason we are able to do this is because when Jesus was in trouble, he did not pray for his troubles to go away—praise God! Instead, he prayed that his troubles would be for God's greater glory.

What will you do when trouble comes—when it comes to the world and comes to you? Sooner or later, you will find yourself saying what Jesus said: "Now is my soul troubled." The question is, What will you say next? What will you ask God to do? Our Savior does not teach us to say, "Father, save me from this hour," but, "Father, glorify your name."

8

"We Are Afflicted in Every Way"

Paul's Light and Momentary Troubles

(2 Corinthians 4:7–18)

It was after the death and resurrection of Jesus Christ, during a missionary journey somewhere in the Roman world, and Paul was in trouble. Real trouble. In truth, we could say this about almost any city the apostle ever visited, on any mission trip that he ever took. It happened everywhere from Antioch to Rome: wherever Paul went, sooner or later he faced persecution for proclaiming the gospel.

The apostle puts his sufferings into perspective in 2 Corinthians 4. On the one hand, Paul is honest about how much trouble he and his friends were facing. In talking about their missionary experience, he uses such words as *afflicted*, *perplexed*, *persecuted*, and *struck down*. Yet he uses each of these words to draw a contrast between their outward troubles and the inward strength God gave to enable them to persevere. "We are afflicted in every way," he says, "but not crushed." Although "perplexed," they are "not driven to despair." They are "persecuted, but not forsaken" and "struck down, but not destroyed" (2 Cor. 4:8–9). Persecution takes Paul to the precipice of what anyone can endure, but no farther.

The apostle also draws a second contrast, between what these earthly troubles feel like right now and what they will look like in the life to come. There is an eternity of difference between the agony we face in this present darkness and the ecstasy we will experience forever in the brightness of God's everlasting glory.

Paul's Troubles

In drawing these contrasts, Paul is talking about a particular kind of trouble. It is not a trouble that everyone faces, nor is it a trouble that we have yet considered, but it is common to the experience of the church in the world. It is the trouble that comes when Christians are persecuted for following Jesus Christ.

If anyone knew what it was like to suffer persecution, it was the apostle Paul. One of the first places he visited as a missionary was Pisidian Antioch. Already by his second Sabbath there, some of the leading men and women of the city "stirred up persecution against Paul" and drove him "out of their district" (Acts 13:50). Next he went to Iconium. That visit lasted a little longer, but eventually Jewish and Gentile leaders in that city, too, conspired against Paul (14:5). So he fled to Lystra, where the crowds "stoned Paul and dragged him out of the city, supposing that he was dead" (v. 19). But the apostle was only "mostly" dead: the next day, he got back up on his feet and continued his missionary journey.

There are more stories about Paul's persecution than there is space to tell in these pages. In Philippi, he was beaten with rods and thrown in prison (16:22–23). In Corinth, he was brought up on false legal charges before being acquitted (18:12–17). In Ephesus, there were huge riots against the Christian gospel (19:21–41). When Paul traveled to Jerusalem, he was arrested while worshiping at the temple. Some of the citizens wanted to beat him to death, and they would have done it, too, except that Roman soldiers appeared on the scene and saved his life (21:27–33).

If these stories were not in the Bible, it might be hard for us to believe some of the startling summaries that Paul gives of the sufferings he faced. On one occasion, he boasted that he had endured "far more imprisonments" than anyone else, "with countless beatings" that left him "often near death" (2 Cor. 11:23). To prove this, he proceeded to list some of the hardships that he had faced:

Five times I received at the hands of the Jews the forty lashes less one. Three times I was beaten with rods. Once I was stoned. Three times I was shipwrecked; a night and a day I was adrift at sea; on frequent journeys, in danger from rivers, danger from robbers, danger from my own people, danger from Gentiles, danger in the city, danger in the wilderness, danger at sea, danger from false brothers; in toil and hardship, through many a sleepless night, in hunger and thirst, often without food, in cold and exposure. (2 Cor. 11:24–27; cf. 6:4–5)

On another occasion, as Paul described the state of the church in the world, he said: "To the present hour we hunger and thirst, we are poorly dressed and buffeted and homeless. . . . We have become, and are still, like the scum of the world, the refuse of all things" (1 Cor. 4:11–13).

The next time we are tempted to think that we have a lot of troubles in life, considering the sufferings of the apostle Paul will help put things into proper perspective.

When Paul talked about his troubles, he wasn't holding a pity party or trying to get people to feel sorry for him. He wasn't bragging about how brave he was, either. He was simply providing a straightforward account of what he had actually experienced.

In a surprising way, Paul was saying that his prayers were answered, because one of his greatest ambitions in life was to share in the sufferings of Christ. When Paul first surrendered his life to Jesus on the Damascus Road, he was told in no uncertain terms how much he would have to suffer for the cause of the gospel (Acts 9:15–16). Paul embraced this. His life prayer was to share in Christ's sufferings, "becoming like him in his death" (Phil. 3:10). He willingly chose to take up a cross for the Savior who died on a troubled cross for him.

This helps to explain why Paul described persecution as a gift: "It has been granted to you that for the sake of Christ you should not only believe in him but also suffer for his sake" (Phil. 1:29). Talk about a gift that nobody wants! Who likes to suffer? Nevertheless, Paul regarded persecution as a privilege of his apostleship—a perfect opportunity to glorify God. He also found joy in the suffering he endured for Christ and his kingdom. In almost every passage where Paul talks about persecution, he also testifies to finding joy in the goodness of God. He is always saying things like "I rejoice in my sufferings" (Col. 1:24) or "I delight . . . in persecutions" (2 Cor. 12:10 NIV). The point is not that Paul enjoyed suffering any more than anyone else does, but that he had a supernatural source of joy in the presence of God the Holy Spirit.

The Persecuted Church

Paul has much to teach us about what to do when trouble comes. Perhaps few Christians will ever suffer anything close to what this man endured. Nevertheless, the troubles he faced are relevant to our own experience.

Paul's persecution is relevant, first, because it helps all of us count the high cost of Christian discipleship. Understand this: a decision to *live* for Christ is also a decision to *die* for Christ. If we know what some Christians have suffered, then we can be sincere in our commitment to follow Christ, no matter what.

What Paul endured is especially relevant for anyone who is called to live in one of the world's hardest places in the name of Jesus and share the gospel. But even if we do not go to one of the world's hardest places, we may still find ourselves in some tight spots. For example, a college student may go home for the summer and spend time with friends from high school. It is a lot easier to go along with the crowd than to put up with the comments that people always make when a believer decides not to say what other people are saying, not to do what they are doing, or not to laugh about what they are laughing about when what they say, do, and laugh about is not honoring to God. Or, to give another example, a Christian employee may serve in a workplace where there is a very real temptation to keep Christianity quiet. The subtle but unmistakable result of giving in to this temptation is to turn a *personal* relationship with Jesus Christ into a *private* relationship with Jesus Christ. Paul's example challenges every Christian to take a stronger stand.

What the apostle suffered is also relevant because it reminds us of the real persecution that the church is suffering around the world today. It is easy to focus on what is happening in America or the West and to miss what is happening in other countries. According to the annual World Watch List compiled by Open Doors, more than one thousand churches were attacked in one recent year, and more than four thousand Christians were killed.[1]

In Nigeria, the militant Islamic organization Boko Haram announced publicly in 2015 its intention to "cleanse" the country of all Christians. In the words of their leader: "This is a war against Christians. . . . Allah says we should finish them when we get them."[2] Toward that end, jihadist terrorists burned churches, destroyed entire villages, and kidnapped hundreds of teenage girls, most of them Christians. During one week alone, Boko Haram attacked fishing villages on Lake Chad and killed more than two thousand people. Many women and children drowned as they took to the lake in overcrowded boats, which later capsized.[3] Similar attacks took place in Niger, where Islamic protests against the satiric French magazine *Charlie Hebdo* led to the destruction of seventy churches.[4]

Church attacks were even more common in northern Syria, where the Islamic State, also known as ISIS, drove nearly a million Christians from their homes in the autumn of 2014, forcing them to face a winter of deprivation. The same thing happened in northern Iraq, where, on Easter Sunday in 2015—as a result of attempted genocide—the church bells in the historic city of Mosul fell silent for the first time in more than fifteen hundred years. Christian homes in that city were marked with a black letter—"N" for Nazarene.[5] Then there were the horrific executions in Libya, where Muslims beheaded twenty-one Coptic Christians on the shores of the Mediterranean Sea.

To cite yet another example, the Somalian terrorist organization Al-Shabaab attacked Kenya's Garissa University College. The militants separated the Muslims from the Christians by asking them to recite verses from the Quran. Then they murdered the Christian students in cold blood—nearly 150 of them, many the first students in their families to attend college.

We need to be aware of what is happening to the church around the world. The suffering of our brothers and sisters is not accidental; it is intentional. ISIS entitled one of its public calls for genocide "A Message to the Nation of the Cross." Here is its message, according to news broadcasts from the time: "We will conquer your Rome, break your crosses, and enslave your women." As a member of God's cruciform kingdom, we should consider what God is calling us to do in response. Are we praying for the persecuted church? Are we asking God if there is anything that we can do to help?

One college student wrote to ask why the evangelical church is focusing "very little on the crisis and persecution of our brothers and sisters in the Middle East, North Africa and Western Africa." Members of the Jewish community asked the same question. One rabbi observed that if Jews had been beheaded in Libya rather than Christians, the worldwide Jewish community would have been crying out for their family members—their own flesh and blood. Why isn't there more outrage in the church, he wanted to know, and why isn't there a stronger sense of solidarity with our brothers and sisters in the faith?

Necessary Troubles

One way to build a greater sense of solidarity is simply to be aware of the sufferings of the persecuted church. But we also need to understand why God permits his beloved children to suffer and even to die for the sake of his gospel. What is God's purpose in these troubles?

This question was not as hard for Paul as it is for us. The apostle knew exactly why Christians were persecuted everywhere they went, and he understood well that this was part of God's plan. Here is how he explained it: we are "always being given over to death for Jesus' sake." Why? "So that the life of Jesus also may be manifested in our mortal flesh. So death is at work in us, but life in you" (2 Cor. 4:11–12).

In some mysterious way, the pattern of Good Friday and Easter Sunday gets repeated in the experience of the persecuted church. Indeed, this is necessary for the evangelization of the lost. There is something about seeing faithful believers endure suffering for the sake of Jesus Christ that helps unbelievers understand the gospel. They cannot see Jesus hanging on the cross, but they can see a community that shares in his suffering, and

God uses this awful emblem to bring new spiritual life out of death. A church that is marked by the cross through its suffering in the world is a living testimony to the gospel of the risen Christ.

A compelling example from church history occurred in the city of Otranto (near Rome) in 1480. As Christians there desperately defended their homes and their families against Muslim forces, thousands were killed. Of the survivors, the women and children were taken into slavery, while some eight hundred men between the ages of fifteen and fifty were given a choice between converting to Islam or being beheaded. After the city's bishop and archbishop were brutally murdered, a courageous tailor named Antonio Primaldi led the rest of the survivors in defying Islam. They were beheaded one by one. According to Giovanni Laggetto's *Historia della Guerra di Otranto del 1480*, Primaldi said: "We fight to save our souls for our Lord, so that having died on the cross for us, it is good that we should die for him."[6]

Like the worthy citizens of Otranto, many persecuted Christians have seen the connection between their excruciating suffering and the cross of Christ. And many times God has used the courageous witness of martyrs to bring people to faith in Jesus. This explains why Paul was not crushed, driven to despair, feeling forsaken, or destroyed even if he was afflicted, perplexed, persecuted, and struck down. He could see that God was using his sufferings for the salvation of the lost. "As grace extends to more and more people," he said, "it may increase thanksgiving, to the glory of God" (2 Cor. 4:15).

God's saving purpose for the sufferings of his people calls us to a particular kind of prayer: prayer that these sufferings will not be in vain, but will lead to the salvation of the lost. Whenever we hear the sad news that our brothers and sisters are being persecuted, we should not despair. Instead, we are called to believe that this is part of God's purpose and remember to pray for their witness.

On September 12, 2014, Pastor Saeed Abedini wrote a heartfelt letter to his daughter Rebekka on the occasion of her eighth birthday. Abedini wrote the letter from the cell of an Iranian prison, where for years he had been held captive for preaching the gospel of Jesus Christ. In fact, this was the third consecutive year that he would miss his little girl's birthday. He wrote:

> My Dearest Rebekka Grace, HAPPY 8th BIRTHDAY! You are growing so fast and becoming more beautiful every day. . . . Oh how I long to see you. I know that you question why you have prayed so many times for my return and yet I am not home yet. Now there is a big WHY in your mind you are asking: WHY Jesus isn't answering your prayers. . . . The answer to the WHY is WHO. WHO is in control? LORD JESUS CHRIST is in control. . . . Jesus allows me to be kept here for His glory. . . . People die and suffer for their Christian faith all over the world and some may wonder why? But you should know the answer of WHY is WHO. It is for Jesus. He is worth the price.[7]

Help in Trouble

It is evident from Pastor Abedini's testimony that he experienced the same thing that the apostle Paul experienced when he was in prison, namely, the comforting presence of God's Holy Spirit. This, too, should call us to prayer. We may not always be able to alleviate the sufferings of the persecuted church, although sometimes we can. But whether we are able to give our brothers and sisters any practical help or not, we can at least pray for the peace of God's presence.

In 2015, the National Association of Evangelicals expressed its "collective grief and profound concern for the suffering of Christians around the world." The group said, "Our brothers and sisters in Christ are being persecuted, uprooted from their ancestral homes, and even martyred because of their faith." The NAE then called on Christians everywhere "to engage in sustained prayer for those whose lives are threatened, and especially for the family members of the martyrs who have been brutally killed" and "to give generously towards the needs of refugees, and for the rebuilding of shattered communities."[8]

God answers our sustained prayers for Christians under threat by sending the kind of help that he always sends when his people are in real trouble. The Bible says that God is "a stronghold for the oppressed, a stronghold in times of trouble" (Ps. 9:9). In ways that surpass human understanding, the close presence of God the Holy Spirit gives hope in the darkness to the persecuted church. The same Jesus who suffered in anguish on the cross—and therefore knows better than anyone else what it feels like to be in trouble—is with us to save us.

For the apostle Paul, one of the greatest comforts was knowing that whatever suffering he experienced was only temporary, and therefore—in the light of eternity—of only minimal consequence. When we look at the list of the man's troubles, we may well find it hard to believe that he survived at all, let alone stayed faithful to the cause of Christ. On one occasion, he admitted,

"We were so utterly burdened beyond our strength that we despaired of life itself" (2 Cor. 1:8). But in 2 Corinthians 4:17, Paul dismisses all his suffering with a wave of his hand, calling it "this light momentary affliction."

Christian suffering is "momentary" because this life is merely a short prelude to a long eternity. After we die, we will rise again and then live forever. Paul was absolutely certain that the same Holy Spirit "who raised the Lord Jesus will raise us also with Jesus" (2 Cor. 4:14). "We suffer with him in order that we may also be glorified with him," he said (Rom. 8:17). This is why the apostle did not lose heart, even when he was persecuted to the point of death. The resurrection of Christ means the resurrection of the Christian, and therefore we have nothing to lose—only life to gain.

When we rise again, we will enter such unimaginable glory that all of life's troubles will fade away. "For this light momentary affliction," as Paul calls it, "is preparing for us an eternal weight of glory beyond all comparison, as we look not to the things that are seen but to the things that are unseen. For the things that are seen are transient, but the things that are unseen are eternal" (2 Cor. 4:17–18).

As Successful as the Cross

The weighty glory that God has prepared for us is greater than we can imagine—and closer than we think. Writing in the second century after Christ, the Greek philosopher Aristides offered an admiring description of the way that Christians think about death. "If any righteous man among them passes from the world," he wrote, "they rejoice and offer thanks to God; and they escort his body as if he were setting out from one place to another near."[9] This is the right way for Christians everywhere to think about death and life: heaven is near.

The people who really believe this—the people who hold on to the cross and look in hope for God's weighty glory—are the people who do the most good in the world, with the greatest patience and the most endurance.

A notable example comes from the life of Clarence Jordan. A man of unusual ability, Jordan held doctoral degrees in Greek, Hebrew, and agriculture. As gifted as he was, Jordan dedicated his life to serving the poor. In the 1940s, he founded Koinonia Farm in Americus, Georgia—a place where poor whites and poor blacks could live together in Christian community.

A multiracial community such as Koinonia Farm faced severe hostility in the segregated South of the 1940s, much of it from church members. People in town tried everything they could to stop Jordan. They boycotted his produce. They slashed the tires of his workers' automobiles. Finally, one night in 1954, the Ku Klux Klan came and tried to get rid of him once and for all. They set fire to every building on the farm except Clarence's house, which they riddled with bullets.

The next day, a newspaper reporter came out to survey the farm's smoldering remains. To his astonishment, he found Dr. Jordan busily at work in the field, hoeing and planting. "I heard the awful news," the reporter said, "and I came out to do a story on the tragedy of your farm closing."

Jordan kept working the soil while the reporter kept pestering him for a response, finally saying: "Well, Dr. Jordan, you got two of them Ph.D.s and you've put fourteen years into this farm, and there's nothing left of it at all. Just how successful do you think you've been?"

Jordan stopped working, leaned on his hoe, turned to the reporter, looked him straight in the eye, and said, "About as successful as the cross." Then he proceeded to say: "Sir, I don't think you understand us. What we are about is not success but faithfulness. We're staying. Good day."[10]

Honestly, my hope is to be spared from any serious persecution. But if such trouble comes my way, I pray that I will see it as a light and momentary affliction, that my service to Jesus will be as successful in its own way as the cross, and that by faith in the risen Christ, I will gain the eternal weight of his glory. I have the same hope and the same prayer for everyone who reads this book.

Epilogue

Here Comes Trouble!

(John 16:25–33)

So it's a week from now, or a year, or maybe even a decade, and you're in trouble. Real trouble. It's not someone else who's having a lot of difficulty; this time, it's you.

I can't tell you what kind of trouble you'll be in. Maybe you will suffer from a debilitating disease or suddenly face some life-threatening illness. Maybe you will lose someone you love. Maybe you will be overwhelmed by poverty, bloodshed, and the strife of a fallen race. Maybe you will have a crisis of faith, in which suddenly you doubt the saving promises of God in Jesus Christ. Or maybe you will gradually wander away from the Lord until one day you wake up and realize that spiritually you're in a place you never expected to end up.

Whatever your particular situation happens to be, one day you will find yourself repeating the words of the old spiritual:

It's me, it's me, it's me, O Lord,
    Standin' in the need of prayer.
Not my brother or my sister, but it's me, O Lord,
    Standin' in the need of prayer.
Not my mother or my father, but it's me, O Lord,
    Standin' in the need of prayer.
Not the stranger or my neighbor, but it's me, O Lord,
    Standin' in the need of prayer.

Not Surprised by Suffering

How can I possibly know that you will be in trouble?

I could defend this claim *historically* by telling you the stories of other Christians. As a pastor and as a college president, I have heard many tales of woe: chronic illness; the death of close friends or their children; discouragements and doubts; faith lost and not yet recovered; unemployment; anxiety; dreams deferred until finally they were abandoned. These are only some of the stories I could tell, simply based on the lives of people I know.

I could also defend my claim *personally* by telling you about some of my own troubles. My life has been extraordinarily blessed, yet over the years, I have suffered my share of painful trials and carried some heavy burdens. I have had enough trouble to understand what a friend meant when he said to me, "I am in a constant state of suffering pre-perfection."

I could defend my claim *biblically* by going back to Genesis 3, where we read how our first parents ate the forbidden fruit. Then I could show the tragic consequences of their fall into sin, which Job summarized like this: "Man who is born of a woman is few of days and full of trouble" (Job 14:1). Or I could defend my claim *theologically* by talking about the doctrines of original sin, total depravity, and the final judgment—the doctrines that help explain all the troubles in the world.

Instead, I want to make my claim more straightforwardly. I want to defend it *christologically* by quoting the clear words of Jesus, who simply said, "In this world you will have trouble" (John 16:33 NIV).

Jesus spoke these words in the upper room where he shared his Last Supper with his disciples. He knew that his hour had come and that soon he would suffer for the sins of the world. As he looked ahead to the time after he was gone, he knew that his disciples would face one trouble after another. This theme comes up repeatedly in his final discourses. Jesus told his disciples that he was going to leave them (John 13:33, 36; 16:28). He told them that the world would hate them as much as it hated him (John 15:18–19). He told them that people would try to kill them (John 16:2) and that they would weep and lament in sorrow and anguish (John 16:20). He told them that they would abandon him and scatter in every direction (John 16:32). Finally, he summarized all of their tribulation in this simple declaration: "In this world you will have trouble."

Although these words were spoken specifically to the first disciples, they remain relevant today for anyone who hopes to go out and make a difference in the world for Jesus Christ. One thing is certain: trouble is coming your way.

You probably know this already. If you are part of the church, then you know that trouble is common to the people of God. As the president of a Christian college, I am always a little surprised when people talk about the "real world" as something they can experience only when they get off campus. As far as I can tell, we have the same kinds of problems at Wheaton College that people have anywhere. Every year, some of our faculty and staff members and students endure illnesses and suffer the death of close family members. Some face financial hardships—times when they aren't sure how God will provide. Some are harmed by other members of the community or feel that they have been treated unfairly by those in power. There are conflicts over race, theology, sexuality, politics, and religion—all of the world's major struggles. At one point or another, most people in our community feel discouraged, maybe even desperate.

This is not unusual. Indeed, it is the normal experience of God's suffering people in this sinful world. What Jesus said to his disciples has been true for his church down through the centuries: "In this world you will have trouble."

These words seem especially relevant for the church today. One of the main reasons we will have trouble is because we are followers of Jesus Christ. This is really the main point of John 16:33. Our commitments and convictions will be opposed by a culture that seeks its own power and pleasure rather than the honor and glory of God. It is hard to predict where any individual Christian will face this pressure. But the more people say that Christianity is intolerant and immoral, the more tempting it will be to leave Jesus Christ out of the conversation, and thus to try to avoid the trouble that comes to everyone who bears his name.

Take Heart!

In anticipation of your inevitable tribulation, I want to end this book with a message of gospel hope. It is the same message that Jesus gave to his disciples. Yes, he was honest about all of the trouble that they were sure to face, but not for a moment did he regard this as anything for them to be troubled about. In fact, Jesus repeatedly told them *not* to be troubled.

We see this at the beginning of John 14. Jesus had just prophesied that Peter, of all people, would deny him three times that very night. The disciples must have been shocked when they heard this, and their faces probably showed it, because the next thing Jesus said was, "Let not your hearts be troubled" (John 14:1a).

Jesus said the same thing later in the chapter when he was explaining what life would be like for his disciples without him. He knew how dismayed they were every time he said that he was going to leave them—which is something he said repeatedly on the night when he was betrayed. But Jesus reassured them by telling them that he would send them the Holy Spirit, and he encouraged them by saying, "Let not your hearts be troubled, neither let them be afraid" (John 14:27). Simply put, Jesus commands us not to be troubled by our troubles.

We hear the same command in John 16:33, where Jesus said: "In this world you will have trouble. But take heart!" (NIV). This declaration is a divine imperative. Jesus Christ is not merely encouraging us to do something; he is telling us to do it. No matter what troubles may come, do not let your heart be troubled, but take courage instead.

This was not the first time that Jesus had told someone to

"Take heart." The presence of this command in other Gospel narratives (Matt. 9:2, 22; Mark 6:50) gives us the impression that this was one of our Savior's favorite sayings. But this time it came with a promise. Jesus gave us an exceptionally good reason to take heart. He said, "In this world you will have trouble." Then he said, "But take heart!" Why? Because "I have overcome the world" (John 16:33 NIV).

What may seem strange about this promise is the verb tense that Jesus used. Remember, Jesus spoke these words the night *before* he died on the cross. He had not yet paid the price for all our sin, offering atonement through his sacrificial blood. He had not yet returned from the grave, rising by the power of the Holy Spirit in a body of immortal splendor. He had not yet ascended to heaven, claiming his place of rule and authority at the right hand of God. Jesus had not yet finished the work that he had come to do. Nevertheless, he said, "I have overcome the world."

As far as Jesus was concerned, the work of our salvation was as good as done. He had already resisted every temptation to sin. So he was fully prepared to offer his life as a perfect sacrifice. Already the momentous events that would lead him onto the cross, into the grave, and then out of the empty tomb had been set in motion. Jesus was looking forward in faith to the day when his promise would come true, when he would overcome the world.

What does this promise mean for us today?

If Jesus has overcome the world, then death has been defeated, the debt of sin has been canceled, and the door is open to eternal life. Therefore, our troubles are only temporary, and whatever suffering we experience will never separate us from the love that God has for us in Jesus Christ.

If Christ has overcome the world, then *we* can overcome the world. We can resist temptation. We can persevere through persecution. We can live for Christ and his kingdom. We can also *die* for Christ and his kingdom, with the full expectation of receiving everything God has promised to people who overcome the world: we will eat from the tree of life (Rev. 2:7), we will sit on heaven's throne (3:21), we will receive the full inheritance of the children of God (21:7), we will see the end of every oppression, and every last tear will be wiped from our eyes (v. 4).

This is why we take heart: it is because Christ has overcome the world. In his sermon on John 16:33, Charles Spurgeon said: "My Lord's words are true as to the tribulation. I have my share of it beyond all doubt." In saying this, Spurgeon surely was referring to his own lifelong struggle with depression, among other hardships. But taking careful note of Christ's command to "be of good cheer," as it says in the old King James Version, the famous preacher wondered aloud what argument his Savior would use to support such a bold command. "Why, it is His own victory," Spurgeon replied. Therefore, we are fighting against an enemy that is already defeated. "O world," he said. "Jesus has already vanquished thee; and in me, by His grace, He will overcome thee again. Therefore am I of good cheer and sing unto my conquering Lord."[1]

The Overcomers

When trouble comes—as it will—I hope and pray that rather than letting your heart be troubled, you will take heart in the promises of God and the overcoming victory of Jesus Christ, who wants to give you his peace.

This is what God's people have done down through the centuries when they were in every kind of trouble you can imagine. Think again of the great men and women of faith whom we have considered throughout this short book—and imagine what they might say if they could testify today about the way God in his grace enabled them to be overcomers.

Isaiah would say: "In the year that King Uzziah died, I was in real trouble. I saw the holy Lord on his high and holy throne, and I was undone. I said, 'Woe is me! I am lost! I am a man of unclean lips.' But take heart, my friends: the Lord overcame all my sin. He took away my guilt and atoned for my transgressions. He touched my filthy lips and made me clean."

Elijah would give us hope in God's healing power. He would say: "It was after I came down from Mount Carmel, where fire fell from heaven and God defeated the prophets of Baal, and I was in real trouble. Queen Jezebel wanted to kill me. I was afraid and ran for my life. I ran about three hundred miles before I stopped. But I couldn't outrun my troubles. At one point, I prayed that God would strike me dead on the spot. But take heart: the Lord overcame my deep depression. He touched me, fed me, and spoke to me in a still, small voice. He gave me the grace to carry on."

Ruth would tell us that when there was a famine in the land and no king to rule over Israel, she was in real trouble. She would say: "I lost my husband and I left my home. I traveled to a far country with nothing to call my own. It was life or death. I had nothing to eat. But take heart: the Lord overcame my grief and my poverty. He sheltered me under his wing. He led me into a field full of barley, where I fell into the arms of my redeemer."

King David had his troubles, too. He would tell us that in the springtime—when kings go out to battle—he was in real trouble. He would say: "I saw a beautiful woman. I shouldn't have given her another look, because I knew she was another man's wife. But I gave in to a deadly temptation and took her for myself. My terrible sin all but destroyed my family. But take heart: the Lord overcame my tragic mistake by giving me the grace to confess my sin. 'This poor man cried, and the LORD heard him and saved him out of all his troubles' (Ps. 34:6). Take my word for it: 'The salvation of the righteous is from the LORD; he is their stronghold in the time of trouble. The LORD helps them and delivers them' (Ps. 37:39–40a)."

The prophet Jeremiah would give a different testimony of God's overcoming grace. He would say: "I was at the temple in Jerusalem, by the Benjamin Gate, and I was in real trouble. I had been preaching the true words of God, but the religious leaders didn't want to hear it, so they beat me up and threw me in jail. I'm ashamed to admit it, but I went through a dark night of the soul, in which I blamed God for all my troubles and told him that I wished I had never been born. But take heart: the Lord conquered my enemies and overcame my despair. He rescued me from prison. He restored my hope and renewed my faith in the promises of his covenant. He is 'my strength and my stronghold, my refuge in the day of trouble' (Jer. 16:19a)."

Mary would tell us that during her betrothal—sometime after the engagement and before the wedding—she was in real trouble. She would say: "You'll never believe this, but an angel came and told me that a child would be conceived in my virgin womb. And when the child was born—the baby Jesus—we had nothing

145

but trouble. Soldiers came to kill my son. We fled to Egypt and we were refugees there before coming back home. My boy grew to become a man. Then he left me behind to go out and do his Father's work. Some people were always against him, until finally they killed him. But take heart: the Lord overcame all the burdens of my troubled soul. He gave me the faith to believe that he can do the impossible. And he did the impossible: he raised my crucified son from the dead with the power of eternal life."

Or consider, finally, the testimony of the apostle Paul. He would tell us that he was in Ephesus, Philippi, Corinth, or someplace like that, and he was in real trouble. He would say, "There I was, in a dark prison," or, "There I was, trying to keep my head above the waves," or, "There I was on the ground, unconscious, lying in a pool of blood." He would say: "All these things happened to me when I was preaching the gospel. Bad things will happen to you, too, if you bear faithful witness to Jesus Christ. But take heart: the Lord Jesus overcame all my tribulation. Through everything that I suffered, he never broke his promise that he would never leave me or forsake me. And when I look at my life in the light of eternity and consider the weight of glory that is waiting for me, none of my light and momentary afflictions is even worth mentioning."

Each of these men and women suffered greatly. If you look back at the Table of Contents, you will see that each of the chapter titles uses a personal pronoun, such as *I*, *me*, *my*, *you*, or *we*. Each of their stories is personal because what these people suffered was personal. But their deliverance was personal, too, so they could offer a personal testimony of God's overcoming grace.

Ready or Not?

As I consider the words of these great men and women of the faith, I wonder what testimony you will give. I wish I could tell you that all your troubles are over. But I am duty-bound to speak the truth, and the truth is that in this world you will have trouble. Don't just take my word for it; believe the words of Jesus Christ. The question is what you will do with your troubles when they come, and how you will trust in God to bring you through.

Sadly, many people are not ready for all the troubles they will face. Out of all the books that people read on Kindle, one quotation is highlighted more than any other, by a margin of two to one. It's a sentence from *The Hunger Games*, which reads: "Because sometimes things happen to people and they're not equipped to deal with them."[2] Indeed.

Things will happen to you, too—things you may not feel totally ready to deal with. But God has grace for you in Jesus Christ. He will guide you where he wants you to go. He will provide everything you need. He will forgive your sins, redeem your mistakes, and comfort your sorrows. He will restore your soul and renew your spirit. If necessary, he will save your life. He will help you grow in grace and give you something useful to do in the world—something to honor God and serve other people. So your Savior says to you: "Take heart! I have overcome the world" (John 16:33).

If you believe this promise, then when trouble comes, you will be able to pray in faith the way that David did: "For your name's sake, O LORD, preserve my life! In your righteousness bring my soul out of trouble!" (Ps. 143:11). And when you pray for help, God will answer your prayer and deliver you from all your troubles.

Study Guide

Prologue: Nobody Knows the Trouble I've Seen

It's not really a question of *whether* we will have trouble—merely *when*. Jesus promised that in this fallen world, we will experience trouble. That's a result of the fall and also of our status as citizens of heaven, who are reborn in Christ and strangers to this world. In fact, if we are living for Christ, we will experience even more trouble than if we are not. With that thought in mind, it is wise for us to prepare ourselves ahead of time rather than waiting until we're in trouble to develop a strategy for dealing with it.

1. Dr. Ryken describes a time of trouble from his own life. What aspects of his experience can you relate to? Have you had similar feelings or witnessed them in someone close to you? Share your experience.

2. We all have troubles in life. What strategies have helped you get through tough times?

3. What blessings has God given you during times of trouble, and what have you learned about God and about yourself through suffering?

4. Read Psalm 37:39–40. List what God does and what the righteous do. What do you learn from comparing these two lists?

5. What are some practical ways to take refuge in God? What would this look like in your daily life?

Chapter 1: "Woe Is Me!"

Israel was in deep trouble due to the king's sin. It was a godless time. Yet God in his mercy offered them hope and help through the prophet Isaiah, his mouthpiece. The rebellious people of God had the opportunity to hear a revelation straight from God. The message didn't seem very hopeful at first. In fact, it felt as if God was going to send judgment rather than deliverance. The people of God had to understand their situation rightly before they could be led out of it. That's true of us, too: we have to face the depth of our trouble before we can receive God's offer of grace. But when we confess our sin, acknowledging it for what it is—rebellion against God—and turning away from it, God is faithful and just to forgive us and cleanse us.

1. What is one area of your life in which it is easy for you to submit to God? What area of life is more difficult for you to turn over to him?

2. Dr. Ryken lists six woes that Isaiah pronounced on Israel in Isaiah 5: woes for unjust affluence, drunkenness, dishonesty, moral relativism, intellectual pride, and injustice. Discuss ways you see the same sins lived out in your culture, your church, and your own life.

3. Read Isaiah 6:1–7. Describe what Isaiah was experiencing through his senses—sight, sound, touch, smell, and taste. What aspects of his description are particularly vivid or surprising to you?

4. Isaiah's response to experiencing God's awesome holiness was deep repentance. What specific sin or sins did he need to confess? What can we learn about sin and repentance from his confession?

5. The prophet Isaiah may have thought that sins of the tongue were far down the list of things he needed to confess, yet sinful speech is the area where God convicted his conscience. For what sin have you been surprised to experience the Spirit's conviction? What circumstances led you to realize your downfall in that area?

6. Isaiah had the benefit of entering the very throne room of God, and this prompted his repentance. How regularly do you meditate on the character and holiness of God, giving him space to work in your heart? What settings or practices help you to contemplate God's holiness?

7. When was the last time you gave God permission to convict you of sin in the areas where you feel least vulnerable? What sin do you need to deal with before you can fulfill God's calling and experience more of his blessing in your life? How can you make repentance a more regular discipline in your spiritual life?

8. What principles of divine forgiveness can you glean from Isaiah 6:6–7?

Chapter 2: "I've Had Enough"

Anyone and everyone can fall into deep discouragement. Even the most staunch defenders of the gospel can get to the point where they want to give up, where they even wonder if God is real. The question is what we will do with our doubt—will we take it to God and wait for him to help us, or wallow in our bad feelings? Elijah's story teaches us that if we will seek God, he will help us find a way out of our trouble by revealing himself to us.

1. What emotions or circumstances are the greatest threats to your faith? What kinds of experiences are most likely to send you into a cycle of discouragement and doubt?
2. What do you do—whether healthy or unhealthy—when you are discouraged or doubtful? What are some things you *should* do in those dark times? What activities or disciplines might renew your spirit and help you experience God's grace in times of trouble?
3. Read 1 Kings 19:1–10. Here we find the prophet Elijah at a point of extreme discouragement. Looking back at the preceding chapters, as well as considering this passage, what factors may have contributed to Elijah's spiritual depression? Which of these factors have been causes of discouragement and doubt in your own life?
4. What did Elijah do when he was discouraged? Which of his actions are instructive for us, as an example to follow? Is there anything in his actions that serves as a warning for us—something we should be careful not to do when we are discouraged?
5. Read the rest of the story in 1 Kings 19:11–21. List all of the ways that God cared for Elijah (look back at vv. 5–7 also). What does this list teach us about God's character? What principles can you learn from Elijah's experience about God's care for his people during times of discouragement and seasons of despair?
6. What results do you see in Elijah's life from his interactions with God? What changes do you see from verse 4 to the end of the chapter?

7. What practical advice does this passage offer us in dealing
    with discouragement? In helping others walk through a sea-
    son of depression?

Chapter 3: "Where You Die I Will Die"

Sometimes all we can see is the darkness of our circumstances
or the myriad ways life has been unkind to us. Our perspective
gets distorted and diminished. But the story of Ruth urges us
to look beyond what we can see to the possibility that God has
something better in store. We may not get to see the good things
God is doing in this life, as Ruth eventually did, but we can trust
that God will redeem all things for his glory in the end. Our job
is simply to hang onto that truth and rest our hope in God's
character and promises.

1. Dr. Ryken quotes the following prayer: "We are called, sim-
    ply, to hold on to Christ and his cross with one hand . . .
    and to hold on to those we are called to love with the other
    hand . . . with courage, humor, self-abandonment, creativity,
    flair, tears, silence, sympathy, gentleness, flexibility, Christ-
    Likeness." Think of this prayer as a mission statement for
    Christians who are called to help people when trouble
    comes. Is there anything missing from the prayer that might
    also help someone who is grieving? In what ways would
    praying this way and loving this way provide an answer for
    the suffering and violence we see in the world around us?

2. Read Ruth 1:1–14 and try to set the scene: What troubles
    did Ruth face? Do you know anyone with similar struggles?
    What can you do this week to show compassion to someone
    who is poor, disadvantaged, or grieving?

3. Based on Ruth 1:15–22, what were the practical consequences—both long- and short-term—of Ruth's choice to
   stay with Naomi? What does her speech in verses 16–17
   reveal about her character and priorities?
4. Has there been a specific point in life when you made the decision to go wherever God calls you? Share your experience.
   If you haven't made that decision, what is holding you back?
5. We also face smaller decisions in life, some of which have
   long-term consequences. Have you ever faced the kind of
   choice that Ruth had to make, to stay somewhere or go
   somewhere? What did you decide, and what were the short-
   and long-term consequences?
6. Dr. Ryken describes Aelred of Rievaulx's three categories
   of friendship: carnal (let's party!), worldly (mutual advantage), and spiritual (let's help each other follow Jesus). Think
   of a friendship that falls into each category. What influ-
   ence—whether positive or negative—did each friend have
   on your life?
7. Do you think it is possible to have many spiritual friendships
   of the type that Ruth and Naomi shared, or are such friendships rare? Explain your answer. If you don't have a true
   spiritual friendship, brainstorm some ways to go about finding a friend—and becoming a friend—who leads a friendship closer to Jesus.
8. As you think about the rest of the story (read chapters 2–4
   to refresh your memory or to learn what happened to Ruth
   and Naomi), what benefits did these two women receive as a
   result of their relationship? How did their friendship become
   a blessing to others?
9. As you reflect on your own friendships, what steps do you
   think God is calling you to take to become a better friend

to someone? Is there a relationship that you would like to move into the spiritual category? What is a good next step toward that goal?

Chapter 4: "You Are the Man!"

No person—even the strongest leader—is immune to sin. In fact, Satan seems to save his worst attacks and most devious temptations for those who are effective ministers of the gospel. David's story reminds us that each little choice we make is leading us down a path, either toward obedience or sin. The little things matter. But if we've chosen the wrong path, even if we've ended up in a place we never thought we would, there is always hope. We are never outside of God's ability to save us.

1. Sadly, and inevitably, some prominent Christian leaders have public downfalls related to personal sin. What factors can lead godly people into devastating sin?
2. From what you know of David's story, what did God do—and what did David do—during the years between his calling to the kingship and his ascension to the throne? What experiences and habits formed him into a good and godly leader?
3. Dr. Ryken points out that even if we do all the right things and have every spiritual advantage, we can still give in to deadly temptation. What signs do you see that you are in spiritual danger? What specific protective actions can you take in light of the constant danger you are in?
4. Read 2 Samuel 11:1–17. What were the causes of David's downfall? What warning signs did he ignore? What actions could he have taken along the way to prevent his transgressions?

5. Contrast Uriah's behavior with David's. What did Uriah do differently? What factors helped him remain blameless, whereas David sinned?

6. What strategies did Nathan use in 2 Samuel 12:1–14 to help David see his sin? Have you ever had to confront someone about his or her sin? What were the results—whether positive or negative—both in your life and in the life of the person you confronted? What principles can you draw from Nathan's handling of David's situation that might help you in a similar circumstance in the future?

7. In this story, where do you see God's judgment? His mercy? In what ways did God help David in his time of greatest trouble?

8. Looking at David's experience of temptation, sin, and repentance, as well as Nathan's wise spiritual leadership, what lessons do you learn that should affect your life this week? What temptation do you need to guard against? What sin do you need to confess? What person needs to hear a message of God's holiness and mercy this week?

Chapter 5: "Cursed Be the Day I Was Born!"

Success in ministry doesn't always look like success. We may work many years for a single conversion. We may feel as if more people are being turned away from the gospel than are being turned toward it. But when we are tempted to despair, Jeremiah's story reminds us that our faith rests on the God who is unseen. What is seen is temporary, while what is unseen is eternal. As we struggle to see the unseen with our limited, earthbound vision, God welcomes our cries for help, our songs of praise, and our faith—however faltering—in his promises.

1. What do you believe that God has called you to do in the world? Where, as Frederick Buechner famously said, do "your deep gladness and the world's hunger meet"?

2. Read Jeremiah 20:7–18. What troubles did Jeremiah face?

3. How would you describe the prophet's state of physical, spiritual, and emotional well-being? Which phrases express feelings that you have experienced? What circumstances led to these feelings?

4. Jeremiah went to God with his doubts. What surprises you about his prayer? Is this level of honesty easy or difficult for you to express when you talk with God?

5. Why do you think Jeremiah expressed faith in verses 11–13 and then returned to despair? What can this teach us about prayer and praise? About faith and doubt in the life of a believer?

6. What divine attributes does Jeremiah praise in verses 11–13? What promises of God does he recall? What actions does he trust God to take?

7. Even people who have a strong sense of calling—like Jeremiah—are not immune to seasons of apparent futility, when they are doing all the right things but life is hard and ministry seems fruitless. What disciplines of faith have helped you persevere through seasons of doubt?

8. Write a brief confession of faith that applies specifically to your current circumstances, and use it to guide your mind and heart as you pray in coming days.

Chapter 6: "A Sword Will Pierce Your Own Soul Too"

Mary found herself thrust into a big job that she hadn't signed up for. The news that she would be an unwed teenage mother would have been even worse for her than it is in our day, possibly even endangering her life. Yet she submitted to God's call, willingly taking on a task that would require skills and courage she didn't yet have. In the end, that's all God asks of us—that we respond to him with the words "let it be to me according to your word" and trust that he will equip us for the tasks he puts before us.

1. What are your favorite parts of the Christmas story—the scenes that you treasure year after year?

2. We usually think of Mary as blessed, and indeed she was. But she also experienced deep agony as the mother of Jesus. What troubles did Mary face that every mother faces? What heartaches were unique to her calling as the mother of the Savior?

3. Read Luke 1:26–38. What emotions does Mary express in this passage?

4. What promises does God (speaking through his angel) make to Mary?

5. Read Mary's poem of praise in Luke 1:46–55. What attributes of God does Mary celebrate?

6. In what ways is Mary's psalm similar to your own praise? In what ways is it different? What lessons can you draw from this passage to inform your devotional life?

7. What factors enabled Mary to respond to God in submission when he announced his plan to turn her life upside down? How do you think you would have responded at the same age, or today? What things can you do to better position yourself to respond to God in faith even when he asks you to do something difficult?

8. Is there a challenging task that God is calling you to complete or a step of faith he is calling you to make? Will you respond as Mary did—with joyful and willing obedience?

Chapter 7: "Now Is My Soul Troubled"

We are naturally wired to desire justice. Just think of the young child's plea, "It's not fair!" or the delight we feel when a villain gets what he deserves. Yet the best news ever given was a triumph of injustice—Jesus, the sinless and holy God-man and Creator, dying on behalf of his sinful, rebellious creatures. Justice would have meant getting the deadly punishment we deserve for our sin: death. Justice would have been Jesus remaining in heavenly glory. But Jesus took on flesh and died for us. His "sorrow unto death" rescues us from our ultimate trouble—the deadly consequences of sin.

1. Have you ever been in trouble that you didn't deserve? What did you do? How did you respond?
2. Read John 12:27–28. What troubles was Jesus facing? How is his suffering relevant to your own life?
3. What aspects of Jesus's prayer would have surprised the crowds who heard it? How is his prayer an example of the way we ought to pray?
4. Jesus's prayer was a lament. Read another prayer of lamentation in Psalm 88. What troubles that the psalmist describes were also troubles that Jesus faced? Have you suffered any similar trials? If so, how did you pray about them?
5. Psalm 88 is a brutally honest prayer. What are the benefits of this level of honesty? Is there ever a time when it is not a good idea to pray this way?
6. What expressions of faith do you see in Psalm 88? In John 12:27–28?
7. Read Hebrews 4:14–16. What difference does it make to your life right now that Jesus has firsthand knowledge of your struggles? How might these verses inform and transform your prayer life?

Chapter 8: "We Are Afflicted in Every Way"

When he was converted, the Saul who had created trouble for Christians became the Paul who was in big trouble for being a Christian. It was quite a reversal. Many of us need a similarly miraculous transformation to be able to view the trials and persecutions we face as a gift rather than a curse. Are you willing to pray that your perspective will be altered in this way? Are you open to the possibility that your troubles are working a greater good than you can imagine?

1. Have you ever been persecuted for the cause of Christ or suffered in some way for your Christian convictions? Describe your experience. What impact did the experience have on your spiritual life?

2. According to passages such as John 12:24–26, Philippians 3:10, and 1 Peter 2:20–23, how should we view suffering for our faith?

3. Paul viewed persecution as a gift (2 Cor. 12:10; Col. 1:24). What did he believe about God and about himself that enabled him to think of his extreme difficulties as a privilege?

4. How can we become better educated about the persecution that fellow believers are experiencing around the world? Why is it important to know what is happening to our brothers and sisters? How should we respond when we hear news reports of Christians being abused or even martyred for their faith?

5. List the words that Paul uses in 2 Corinthians 4:7–15 to describe his circumstances. Which of these words can you identify with?

6. Notice what Paul does in response to his dire circumstances in verse 13. When you are intimidated for being a Chris-

tian, how do you usually respond? How can you encourage people who are being persecuted for their faith in Christ to speak out all the more?

7. Paul's boldness came from his faith in what God can do. According to verses 12–15, what good does God bring out of the persecution of believers? How have you seen this exemplified, either in your own life or in the testimonies you have heard from other Christians?

8. Read about the source of our hope in 2 Corinthians 4:16–18. What are some practical ways you can keep this long view in mind when you are suffering or when you are struggling in prayer for fellow believers?

Epilogue: Here Comes Trouble!

Hopefully, the stories in this book have helped you see your own troubles in a new way and prepared you for the troubles you will face in the future. Hopefully, they have shown how God helps us in all our troubles—comforting us with his presence, using our struggles for good, and giving us opportunities to use our pain to comfort others. In this world, we will face troubles, but we can take heart because Jesus has overcome the world.

1. If you could know what will happen to you in the next few years, would you choose to find out? Why or why not?

2. In John 14, what does Jesus promise he will do for his disciples in the future? What promises does he make for the present—for life here on earth?

3. According to this passage, how does God help us in times of trouble?

4. Based on John 14, what actions should we take during seasons of difficulty in the Christian life?

5. Thinking back over the lives of Isaiah, Elijah, Ruth, David, Jeremiah, Mary, Jesus, and Paul, what lessons have you learned about facing trouble that you would like to carry with you in the days ahead? Which person's story has touched or challenged you the most?

6. What is your testimony of being delivered from doubt, discouragement, or depression? How has God helped you in times of trouble?

7. What can you do now to prepare yourself to stand firm in the faith the next time it becomes more difficult to trust God's plan?

Notes

Prologue: Nobody Knows the Trouble I've Seen

1. George Herbert, "Joseph's Coat," in John Drury, *Music at Midnight: The Life and Poetry of George Herbert* (Chicago: University of Chicago Press, 2013), 356.
2. Brian Pusser, "AGB-UVA Symposium on Research and Scholarship in Higher Education," *Occasional Paper No. 41* (Washington, DC; Association of Governing Boards of Universities and Colleges, September 2000), 13–14.
3. Charles Haddon Spurgeon, *Metropolitan Tabernacle Pulpit*, vol. 27 (London: Passmore & Alabaster, 1881), 1595.
4. From the hymn "Jesus, Priceless Treasure" by Johann Franck, 1653.
5. C. H. Spurgeon, *Metropolitan Tabernacle Pulpit: Containing Sermons Preached and Revised,* vol. 35 (Pasadena, TX: Pilgrim Publications, 1969), 260.

Chapter 1: "Woe Is Me!"

1. Aleksandr I. Solzhenitsyn, *The Gulag Archipelago, 1918–1956*, trans. Thomas Whitney and Harry Willetts, abr. Edward Ericson (New York: Harper & Row, 1985), 75.
2. Johannes Kepler, *The Harmony of the World*, quoted in Karl W. Giberson, *The Wonder of the Universe: Hints of God in Our Fine-Tuned World* (Downers Grove, IL: InterVarsity Press, 2012), 201.

Chapter 2: "I've Had Enough"

1. For more information on the warning signs of suicide and what to do about them, contact the National Suicide Prevention Lifeline at 800-273-TALK (8255).
2. Jonathan Blanchard, quoted in Clyde S. Kilby, *A Minority of One: The Biography of Jonathan Blanchard* (Grand Rapids, MI: Eerdmans, 1959), 87.

3. Donald Hall, "Kill the Day," in *White Apples and the Taste of Stone: Selected Poems, 1946–2006* (Boston: Houghton Mifflin, 2006), 390.

4. Don Baker, with Emery Nester, *Depression: Finding Hope and Meaning in Life's Darkest Shadow* (Portland, OR: Multnomah, 1983), 16.

5. Charles H. Spurgeon, *The Soul Winner* (New York: Revell, 1895), 286–87.

6. Rachel Rim, "A Creed for Myself" (January 12, 2015), as posted on her blog, *No Language but a Cry*, https://pilgrimsearch.wordpress.com/2015/01/12/a-creed-for-myself/, accessed June 30, 2015

7. F. W. Krummacher, in R. Larry Todd, ed., *Mendelssohn and His World* (Princeton, NJ: Princeton University Press, 1991), 129.

Chapter 3: "Where You Die I Will Die"

1. Sharon Ohnemus, "When I Lost My Husband," http://www.kilcrease.com/files/Article_Video/When%20I%20Lost%20My%20Husband.pdf, accessed September 30, 2014.

2. Desmond Tutu, "Litany," in *An African Prayer Book* (New York: Doubleday, 2006), 88–90.

3. This prayer is drawn partly from N. T. Wright, *For All God's Worth: True Worship and the Calling of the Church* (Grand Rapids, MI: Eerdmans, 1997).

4. Rose Thurgood, "A Lecture of Repentance," quoted in John Drury, *Music at Midnight: The Life and Poetry of George Herbert* (Chicago: University of Chicago Press, 2013), 16.

5. Francis Bacon, "Of Friendship," in *The Essays or Counsels, Civil and Moral, of Francis Bacon* (Chicago: Donahue, Henneberry, & Co., 1883), 125.

6. Aelred of Rievaulx, *On Spiritual Friendship*, Cistercian Fathers Series: Number 5, trans. Lawrence C. Braceland, ed. Marsha L. Dutton (Collegeville, MN: Liturgical Press, 2010).

7. Ray Bakke, *A Theology as Big as the City* (Downers Grove, IL: InterVarsity Press, 1997), 55.

8. Thurgood, "A Lecture of Repentance," quoted in Drury, *Music at Midnight*, 16.

Chapter 4: "You Are the Man!"

1. Thomas à Kempis, *The Imitation of Christ* (Chicago: Moody Publishers, 2007), 13.13, 55.

2. "Contentment," in *The Valley of Vision: A Collection of Puritan Prayers and Devotions*, ed. Arthur Bennett (Edinburgh: Banner of Truth, 2002), 295.

3. Thomas Watson, *The Ten Commandments* (1692; repr., Edinburgh: Banner of Truth, 1965), 160.

4. Bill Struthers, *Wired for Intimacy: How Pornography Hijacks the Male Brain* (Downers Grove, IL: InterVarsity Press, 2009).

5. John Freeman, "Living in the Shadows: Life as a Game-Player," Harvest USA, http://www.harvestusa.org/living-shadows-life-game-player/#.VcjIrE3bLcg, accessed September 30, 2014.

6. Ibid.

7. David Wolpe, *David: The Divided Heart*, Jewish Lives (New Haven, CT: Yale University Press, 2014), 77.

8. Ibid., 80.

9. Gerald G. May, *Addiction and Grace* (San Francisco: Harper & Row, 1988), 3–4.

Chapter 5: *"Cursed Be the Day I Was Born!"*

1. Kathleen Norris, *The Cloister Walk* (New York: Riverhead, 1996), 31.

2. Ibid., 31–35.

3. John Calvin, *A Commentary on Jeremiah*, 5 vols. (Edinburgh: Banner of Truth, 1989), 3:38.

4. Dietrich Bonhoeffer, *Letters and Papers from Prison*, in Robert Davidson, *Jeremiah*, Daily Study Bible, 2 vols. (Philadelphia: Westminster, 1983), 1:165.

5. R. E. O. White, *The Indomitable Prophet* (Grand Rapids, MI: Eerdmans, 1992), 162.

6. Calvin, *A Commentary on Jeremiah*, 3:44.

7. Derek Kidner, *The Message of Jeremiah: Against Wind and Tide*, The Bible Speaks Today (Downers Grove, IL: InterVarsity Press, 1987), 81.

8. J. G. McConville, *Judgment and Promise: An Interpretation of the Book of Jeremiah* (Leicester, UK: Apollos, 1993), 73–74.

9. Dr. Jones shared this testimony with the Wheaton College Board of Trustees and others.

Chapter 6: *"A Sword Will Pierce Your Own Soul Too"*

1. Thomas Warton the Elder, "Ode on the Passion," in Robert Atwan and Lawrence Wieder, eds., *Chapters into Verse: Poetry in English Inspired by the Bible*, 2 vols. (New York: Oxford University Press, 1993), 2:214–15.

2. Dorothy L. Sayers, *The Man Born to Be King: A Play-Cycle on the Life of Our Lord and Saviour Jesus Christ* (London: Victor Gollancz, 1969), 58–59.

Chapter 7: "Now Is My Soul Troubled"

1. From Rich Mullins, "Hard to Get," © 1998 Liturgy Legacy Music (Admin. by Word Music, LLC), Word Music, LLC. All rights reserved. Used by permission.
2. David Powlison, "I'll Never Get Over It: Help for the Aggrieved," *Journal of Biblical Counseling*, vol. 28, no. 1 (2014), 8–27.
3. John Calvin, *Commentary on Philippians-Colossians* (Grand Rapids, MI: Baker, 1979), 191.
4. "The Masai Creed," quoted in Timothy George, "Jesus on Safari: The Legacy of Jaroslav Pelikan," *First Things* (January 26, 2015), http:// www.firstthings.com/web-exclusives/2015/01/jesus-on-safari, accessed September 30, 2014.

Chapter 8: "We Are Afflicted in Every Way"

1. "2014, the Worst Year Ever for Persecution," *Christianity Today* (March 2015), 14.
2. Quoted in Jamie Dean, "Terror by the Minute," *World* (February 7, 2015), 38.
3. Timothy George, "While Africa Bleeds," *First Things* (February 23, 2015), http://www.firstthings.com/web-exclusives/2015/02/when -africa-bleeds, accessed March 15, 2015.
4. "*Charlie Hebdo* protests destroy scores of churches," *Christianity Today* (March 2015), 16.
5. David Skeel, "Christianity Will Live on in Iraq," *USA Today* (September 22, 2014), http://www.usatoday.com/story/opinion/2014/09/22 /christianity-iraq-persecution-live-return-column/16076311/, accessed September 30, 2014.
6. Matthew E. Bunson, "How the 800 Martyrs of Otranto Saved Rome," *Catholic Answers Magazine* (July 2008), http://www.catholic.com /magazine/articles/how-the-800-martyrs-of-otranto-saved-rome, accessed September 30, 2014.
7. "Pastor's Saeed's Letter to His Daughter Rebekka," Samaritan's Purse, September 26, 2014, http://www.samaritanspurse.org/article/pastor -saeeds-letter-to-his-daughter-rebekka/, accessed September 30, 2014.
8. National Association of Evangelicals, "NAE Stands with Persecuted Church," March 10, 2015, http://nae.net/nae-stands-with-persecuted -church/, accessed March 15, 2015.
9. D. M. Kay, trans., *The Apology of Aristides the Philosopher*, Early Christian Writings, http://www.earlychristianwritings.com/text/aristides -kay.html, accessed September 30, 2014.
10. Recounted in Tim Hansel, *Holy Sweat* (Dallas, TX: Word, 1987), 188–89.

Epilogue: Here Comes Trouble!

1. Charles Spurgeon, "Be of Good Cheer," devotional based on John 16:33 for May 31, *Faith's Checkbook: Being Precious Promises Arranged for Daily Use with Brief Experimental Comments* (Chicago: Moody Press, n.d.), 152.
2. Cited in Mark Shiffman, "Majoring in Fear," *First Things* (November 2014), 19.

General Index

Scripture Index

Also Available from
Phil Ryken

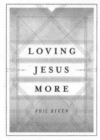

For more information, visit crossway.org.